WELCOME TO MY GARDEN

WELCOME TO MY GARDEN

A Father's Gift of Reflections, Life Lessons, and Advice

BRIAN MURRAY

SACKETS HARBOR PRESS

SACKETS HARBOR PRESS

215 Washington Street, Suite 001
Watertown, New York 13601

Copyright © 2023 by Brian H. Murray

Hardcover ISBN: 978-0-9983816-1-9
Paperback ISBN: 978-0-9983816-5-7
Ebook ISBN: 978-0-9983816-3-3
Audiobook ISBN: 978-0-9983816-4-0

All rights reserved.

Library of Congress Control Number: 2023923504

Cover design by Karl Spurzem
Cover Image by Valenty/Shutterstock.com

"Show me your garden and I shall tell you what you are."
—*Alfred Austin*

TABLE OF CONTENTS

	An Invitation to the Reader	ix
	Opening Letter	xi
CHAPTER 1	Childhood: Recognizing and Untangling the Imprints of Youth	1
CHAPTER 2	Break the Rules: Individuality, Change, and Taking Control of Your Destiny	10
CHAPTER 3	Mindset: Conquering Limiting Beliefs and Unleashing Potential	21
CHAPTER 4	Create: Experiencing the Magic of Being a Creator	30
CHAPTER 5	Delayed Gratification: The Power and Perils of Sacrificing for the Future	37
CHAPTER 6	Discomfort: Overcoming Fear and Doing Hard Things	51
CHAPTER 7	You Are Enough: The Challenge of Knowing, Being, and Loving Yourself	62
CHAPTER 8	Gratitude: A Priceless Treasure Free for the Taking	73

TABLE OF CONTENTS

CHAPTER 9	Health Span: Living the Longest, Happiest, and Healthiest Life	80
CHAPTER 10	Spirituality: The Things That Are Unseen	88
CHAPTER 11	Empathy: The Essence of Our Humanity	98
CHAPTER 12	Generosity: The Selfless Virtue	107
CHAPTER 13	Mortality: The Ephemeral Nature of Life	114
CHAPTER 14	Mindfulness: The Miracles All around Us	124
CHAPTER 15	Positivity: A Cornerstone of Happiness	136
CHAPTER 16	Conclusion: Closing Thoughts and Wishes	151
	Proud of You by IN-Q	157
	Recommended Reading	161
	Acknowledgments	163
	Endnotes	166

AN INVITATION TO THE READER

Welcome to My Garden was not originally intended for a broader audience. It's a book of life lessons that was written to and for my kids, who are young adults. The idea was to share stories, reflections, and advice with them that I wish someone had shared with me when I was younger. Writing the book was a labor of love. Every time I sat down to write, I visualized one of the kids sitting across from me, attentively listening. I was speaking to them through the written word, and it comes from the heart. It comes from the soul. It comes from a deep and selfless place that any loving parent can understand. As a result, the stories are more personal than I would otherwise have shared. The reflections are more vulnerable. The lessons are more meaningful. And the advice is more heartfelt.

The decision to publish this book was not made until the draft manuscript was nearing completion. Friends who were aware of the project expressed an interest in reading it, suggesting they would find it helpful. Initially, I was taken aback by this request. I tend to be a private person, and *Welcome to My Garden* recounts some of the biggest mistakes I've made in my life. It reveals flaws, hardships, and experiences that are deeply personal. The prospect of sharing something so intimate was unsettling, and it seemed like a terribly difficult choice. But after further reflection, I came to realize that such a decision wasn't really hard at all. Why? Because I was weighing my own discomfort and insecurity against the potential value the book might offer to others. To *you*, the reader. I could either accede to my fears or allow myself to be guided by higher ideals. Looking at it from this perspective, I recognized that I couldn't *not* share the book. Not only would it go counter to my values, but it would be antithetical to the very lessons and virtues espoused in the book itself.

The decision to publish *Welcome to My Garden* did prompt me to make a few alterations, none of which were material to the essence of the work. Since some of the stories are sensitive, in a few cases I have taken the liberty of changing a name or otherwise disguising the identity of people to protect their privacy. But I have preserved the accuracy and details of all events to the best of my ability. If there are any factual errors or pertinent omissions it is unintentional. I would also like to be clear that the reflections and advice tendered herein are based on my personal experiences and opinion and not intended to be taken as absolute truths. My life's journey has instilled an appreciation for diverse perspectives, and I've become acutely aware of the limits of my own knowledge. I encourage you to read the book with equal parts openness and discernment, and take away what resonates with you based on your own values, experiences, and circumstances.

In the Opening Letter that follows, you will learn more about the origin and purpose of *Welcome to My Garden*. It was created to take my kids on a tour. A tour of life experiences designed to impart the most important and timeless lessons I've learned. A tour that you are now invited to go on with us. And while the original intent of the book was to provide enrichment and make a positive difference in the lives of my children, I sincerely hope that it can do the same for you.

OPENING LETTER

Dear Alexa, Jackie, Ryan, and Kyle,

As I write this letter, I'm about six months removed from a trip to Nepal, where I had the opportunity to explore Kathmandu and trek through the Khumbu region to Everest Base Camp, staying in the villages along the way, visiting monasteries, and witnessing the incredible beauty of the Himalayas. I found Nepal to be a spiritual place, and I was fortunate to share the journey with some wonderful travel companions: a group of fifteen people who started the trip as strangers but became close friends as the wonders and trials of the expedition unfolded. The entire adventure was a magical experience that made a deep impact on me. In part, this was because the trip provided a unique opportunity for personal growth and time for reflection. Pulling myself out of my everyday routine, unplugging, living simply, and spending an extended time in such an immersive environment helped quiet my mind and create a rare chance to examine my life from a different perspective—as if I was outside looking in.

When I reflect on my professional life to date, I could say that I've achieved success by almost any objective measure. And while I can take pride in what I've accomplished, I have come to realize that professional achievements, regardless of how grand, do not provide as much personal fulfillment as most people would expect. My vocation has been a part of my self-identity for a long time, but that part fades and seems less relevant with each passing day. I now know that work-related attainments and material possessions are a byproduct of what I've done as opposed to who I am, and I appreciate more than ever that other things in life are far more important.

I have so much to be grateful for. Yet when I reflect back on my life to this point, it is being a father that stands out as the most precious gift I've ever received. I take so much pride in who each of you has become. I've supported you and watched with wonder as you've grown into beautiful young adults, and yet I am reluctant to take much credit for that. In my eyes, you've all blossomed from within, and it's been a blessing to witness.

Parenthood. It's a privilege and responsibility unlike any other. The opportunity to be a father and stepfather, while not always easy, has brought me more joy and purpose than anything else in life. For a mother or father, time with our children is precious and fleeting. It's beautiful. It's fulfilling. It can also be painful, confusing, and overwhelming. While I've done the best I can to be a good parent, I can be my own worst critic. As is the case for most parents, I sometimes find myself filled with doubt and wishing I could have done more for you. That I could have been better.

One of the greatest and most unfortunate ironies of parenthood is that for many of us, the most valuable lessons are learned in the later stages of life, after our children are already adults. It might seem strange to you, but when we become parents and welcome our children into the world, we are in many ways still kids ourselves—trying desperately to figure out life at the same time we're frantically navigating the challenges and responsibilities of parenthood, all the while maintaining a facade so that it will look like we know what we're doing. But despite any efforts to mask it from others, the messiness, confusion, and struggles are real, and everyone experiences them.

Over the course of my life and career I've suffered hardships and failures, and made *so many* mistakes: as a parent, as a spouse, and as a human being. Fortunately, such experiences can have a positive aspect—they teach us lessons. They plant seeds from which a garden of wisdom can grow. As physician and author Larry Dossey observed, "The garden is a metaphor for life. It is a place of potential, beauty, abundance, challenge, and transformation. Gardening is a symbol of the spiritual path. It teaches us about patience, perseverance, and the importance of nurturing our own growth." At this stage in my life, I've embraced the cultivation of my own metaphorical garden. I am open. I pursue understanding and truth. I find myself more introspective and contemplative, and I seek spiritual growth and enlightenment. I have learned to tend my garden with great care, breathing new life into dormant seeds while also planting new ones. I water the seeds by reflecting on and learning from my experience. I strive to keep my garden healthy, weeding out what's detrimental, and diligently laboring to transform the trials and tribulations of my life into something beautiful: a garden of wisdom that I can share and, in doing so, perhaps bring a touch of goodness into the world.

The experiences I've had and the mistakes I've made are a part of me. They have shaped me and made me who I am today, and I have nothing but gratitude for that. There is little value in harboring regrets, other than perhaps that they can serve as a reminder of what we can do better moving forward. And that brings me back to my trek, and the nascence of this book. During my time in Nepal, I experienced a number of moments that I would consider to be transcendent. It started with a breath-work exercise led by one of the trip's orchestrators, Mike Posner, that triggered a powerful emotional response. This was followed by other interactions and trials over subsequent weeks that touched me deeply in different ways. None of these things were expected. I did the trek because I wanted to learn about the Nepali culture and witness the majesty of the Himalayas. And while the culture and sights certainly didn't disappoint, it was the people, challenges, and spiritual aspects of the trip that were most profound. In its totality, the journey was life changing, and out of it came a clarity of purpose and direction that included a conviction to write this book. I realized that it's not too late to share with you some of the most meaningful life lessons I've learned so far. To impart some of the knowledge and wisdom that I have accumulated. To give you a tour of the garden I've been cultivating.

I want you to know that I love you very much, and I couldn't be prouder. It's a pride that's rooted in who you are at your core, and not in what you do. That will never change. Each of you has a unique energy and light that shines from within and brightens the world around you. Thank you for being you—I'm grateful for you beyond measure. This book is my gift to you. A gift that was born in one of the most magical, spiritual places in the world. A gift that I am thankful to have the opportunity to share. Life can be so wonderful. But it can also be hard. It can be messy and difficult to navigate. I know you've already faced plenty of challenges, and I know there will be many more to come. It is my sincerest hope that you'll pull something of value from this book that helps you along the rest of your journey.

In the chapters that follow, I'll share a curated collection of personal life experiences. Things that have shaped me and helped me to grow. Seeds from which my garden has emerged. In each case, I offer my humble reflections, what I learned, and what I want for each of you. If even one of the stories, lessons, or offerings of advice makes a positive difference in your life, then this book will have fulfilled my greatest wishes, and I will consider it an unqualified success.

Welcome to my garden.

Dad/Brian 2023

1

CHILDHOOD

Recognizing and Untangling the Imprints of Youth

> All of us carry around countless bags of dusty old
> knickknacks dated from childhood: collected resentments,
> long lists of wounds of greater or lesser significance,
> glorified memories, absolute certainties that later turn out
> to be wrong. Humans are emotional pack rats.
> —*Marya Hornbacher*

> I am not what happened to me. I am what I choose to become.
> —*Carl Jung*

It was a warm summer afternoon, and I was riding my bike home. I was thirteen years old and had just finished hanging out at my friend's house—listening to music, talking, and enjoying one of the last days of summer break. With my legs vigorously pumping the pedals and the wind whipping through my hair, I felt like I was flying. I loved to swerve my bike back and forth, hop over potholes, and lift my hands off the handlebars, holding my arms out at my sides like a bird soaring in the sky. Riding my bike, exploring in the woods, and playing with friends were my escapes. It was at moments like this that I felt the happiest and most carefree.

Less than a quarter mile from my house I caught sight of a beat-up Volkswagen Beetle coming from the opposite direction. It was going too fast and kicking up a thick cloud of dust as it barreled down the dirt road. As the car drew closer, I could hear loud music emanating from its open windows. And when it passed, I caught a whiff of pot and saw that there were some older kids inside. I felt a pit in my stomach when I recognized one of them. Mason was a bully from school, and he had it out for me. He hated that I would stand up to him, and I knew that if he spotted me on this desolate stretch of road, things could take a bad turn.

My fears were confirmed when I heard the car skid on the gravelly road behind me. Glancing back over my shoulder, I saw that the driver had slammed on the brakes and was maneuvering an abrupt U-turn, kicking up even more dust. I pedaled frantically, irrationally hoping to get home before they caught me. But within seconds, the car caught up and cut me off, crashing my bike and sending me sprawling. Three boys hopped out of the Volkswagen with bloodshot eyes and wide grins. One was Mason, who, although he was only a year older than me, was an offensive lineman on the school football team and had a good four inches and sixty pounds on me. The other two were several years older, delinquents who I didn't know but had seen lurking in the hallways at school when they weren't skipping or suspended.

Mason didn't waste any time, spewing crude insults and stepping up to shove me with both hands. Despite the futility of my situation, I confronted his aggression with my own, raising my fists and squaring off with him. "Let's go," I said with false bravado. Although Mason was much bigger than me, he was also slower than I was. We both landed some blows and warily circled each other. Having held my own in the initial exchange, I felt a flicker of hope that I wouldn't get pummeled—Mason's grin was gone. He was breathing heavily, and I saw a hint of concern as trickles of sweat began to run down his puffy face. But any glimmer of hope on my part was quickly extinguished when his older friends, growing impatient, decided they were no longer content to stand by and watch. They surged at me from both sides and grabbed my arms. With one of them on either side restraining me, I was defenseless as Mason now smiled crazily and delivered repeated blows to my head and stomach until I felt woozy and began to collapse. They dropped me to the ground, a bloody mess. I curled up in a ball sobbing and covered my head with my arms as the three of them proceeded to kick me from all sides. Laughing and apparently satisfied with their handiwork, they spit on me for good measure, then piled back into their dilapidated car and drove off, shouting obscenities.

After they left, I lay on the side of the road—crying, angry, and ashamed. I could taste blood and dirt in my mouth, and felt one of my eyes starting to swell shut. A mixture of snot and blood drained from my nose and trickled down my chin to my T-shirt, and I felt a sharp pain in my ribs as I sat up. It took me a while to collect myself, but I gradually made my way onto my feet, picked up my bike, and slowly walked home, pushing my bike while leaning on it for support.

My thoughts rapidly turned to the need to hide what had happened from my parents, who I feared would punish me for infractions ranging from fighting to being late to getting blood on my shirt. I was in no condition to withstand the wrath of my father. When I got home I attempted to sneak past my mother, who was busy preparing dinner. But she stopped me, her eyes widening in shock when she saw my bruised and dirty face. She asked what had happened, but I was evasive and quickly went upstairs to clean myself up. When my father arrived home, he spoke to my mother before calling me to the kitchen and demanding answers. I reluctantly told him what had happened, but I downplayed everything as much as possible, assuring him I was fine and it was no big deal. I was surprised when I didn't get in trouble after admitting I had been in a fight—in fact, my parents seemed concerned, which puzzled me. My father even wanted to confront the bullies' parents. While I appreciated their care, it seemed hypocritical. Because the pain from this beating wasn't any worse than what I had sometimes experienced at the hands of my father, dating back to early childhood. And right there hanging on the wall in the kitchen where he was questioning me was a reminder of this—the well-worn leather strap used to deter misbehavior and mete out discipline as he saw fit.

After speaking with my parents, my concerns quickly shifted to whether other kids would find out I had lost a fight, regardless of how lopsided it was. I had learned from experience that if I appeared weak, I would become more of a target for bullying than I already was, and it would keep happening. Any other feelings I had regarding the entire episode were fleeting. For better or worse, by this time in my youth I was becoming somewhat inured to violence and pain. And I had gotten pretty good at stuffing my feelings away. But leaving my feelings unprocessed didn't allow them to pass through me and fade. Instead, like unused possessions getting stored in the basement, they filled up more and more space under the surface. Many years later they would need to be unpacked, examined, and dealt with before I could be free of them.

While there was love in my childhood, it was rarely expressed or demonstrated in healthy ways, I suspect for a variety of reasons. When I was eight, my five-year-old sister Jennifer died of a congenital heart condition. Her illness and passing were devastating for the entire family, but especially my parents. As a father now, I can't imagine the pain of such a loss. Couple that with the fact that my parents were likely operating within the cycle of their own upbringings, and the result was a household that was largely devoid of affection and positive encouragement. My father in particular was highly critical and characterized my involvement in sports and extracurricular activities as a waste of time. I have no recollection of him ever attending an event or offering words of support for anything I did. Instead, there was a lot of stress, intimidation, and misguided attempts on his part to "straighten me out" and "toughen me up" through corporal punishment, hard physical labor, and shaming, among other things painful to recollect. While disciplining kids in such a manner was more commonplace at that time, it sometimes had unintended consequences. Though I usually hid it to protect myself, I was a sensitive child and didn't feel safe in such a harsh environment. My early experiences, both at home and at school, fostered insecurity and hardened me to a point that wasn't healthy, affecting interactions with my younger brother and the world around me. I could have run from Mason and those other kids that beat me up, or at least attempted to de-escalate the situation. But because I was accustomed to hostility and aggression, I leaned into it, a tendency that played out in various forms throughout my youth.

The emotional toll would manifest itself in unhealthy ways for decades. I would frequently find myself in a state of high alert and too easily triggered, making it more difficult to relax, trust, or open up to others. And while the connections between my childhood and some of the challenges I faced as an adult might seem obvious now, for a long time I didn't even recognize that some of my reactions and behaviors weren't normal, let alone what may have caused them. I genuinely thought I was fine. It wasn't until much later in life that I would deliberately reflect on my youth, examining what I experienced with more objectivity and recognizing the lasting effects.

> "The child is in me still and sometimes not so still."
> —*Fred Rogers*

Unpacking everything was a long and difficult process but unquestionably beneficial. With the help of a therapist and a lot of self-education and introspection, I was eventually able to identify and work on the emotional issues and destructive patterns that affected my life and relationships. My higher level of awareness also engendered a sense of responsibility. Blaming anyone or anything outside yourself for your thoughts, feelings, or actions is tricky business and best avoided. It can foster a victim mentality and other unhealthy views, particularly if used to rationalize negativity or unacceptable behaviors. Far better to adopt a sense of agency and focus on doing what's necessary to put yourself on the right path. To forgive and have compassion for those who have caused us harm. As adults, we have the power to make our own choices. I chose to heal, be a better person, and lead a life in closer alignment with my true self. I have also chosen to recognize and be grateful for the blessings in my childhood.

> "It's not what happens to us that matters most,
> it's what we do with our experiences."
> —Edith Eger

There is a strong tendency in all of us to overlook or block out the positive aspects of any life events or relationship where we experience hurt. Author Kent Nerburn captures this sentiment perfectly, noting that "when we leave a situation that has caused us pain, it is tempting to paint that situation with colors of darkness, forgetting the goodness that it offered and the part that it played in the shaping of our life." My parents created positive memories that I cherish—we had some joyous holiday celebrations, summer trips to the Adirondacks, and other fun activities that I greatly appreciated. I am particularly grateful for my mother, who has a kind and generous heart. Finally, unlike so many other children in this world, my basic physical needs were met throughout my childhood, despite financial hardship—primarily as a result of sacrifices made by my parents, who worked hard to see that my siblings and I were provided for. For these and other reasons, I am privileged and grateful for everything I experienced, good and bad. It's all a part of me. It made me the person who I am today.

I have also identified and embraced the positive by-products of my youth. Yes, some of my experiences had undesirable consequences, but they also made me resilient, gritty, and highly empathetic. They played a role in motivating me to achieve lofty professional heights, and they eventually helped me cultivate a higher level of self-awareness and commitment to personal and spiritual growth. From the crucible of trying circumstances can also emerge the capacity to savor gratitude and joy in ways that others may not be capable of.

> "Childhood is a time of great change and upheaval, and it can be a time of great pain and suffering. But it is also a time of great opportunity and growth."
> —Brené Brown

Buddhist philosopher Daisaku Ikeda characterizes the place people grew up and the people who nurtured them as the soil that fosters their growth. And from this soil emerges their ability to "make the flowers of their lives blossom." All aspects of my youth, good and bad, contributed to my growth and development. They are part of the life experiences that seeded and nourished my garden.

Recounting childhood experiences and offering such reflections can be difficult because they're so deeply personal. So why share? Well, I'm certainly not seeking pity or attempting to glorify my experiences in any way. There's nothing to be proud of here, other than the fact that I've chosen a different path and taken the steps necessary to work on myself. That said, I waited far too long to examine my childhood and how it affected me, which I regret. I didn't start therapy until I was in my forties. Sometimes I feel like I spent the first half of my life tying myself up in a jumble of knots, and am now spending the second half detangling them all. The reason that I'm sharing is that I don't want you to make the same mistake I did. Start identifying and untying your own knots sooner. The stakes are too high.

We're *all* influenced by our parental figures and our childhood environments, and the effects can sometimes be lasting and profound, positive or negative, whether we realize it or not. And at our core, we're all still the same little kids living and acting out in adult bodies. The baggage of youth is carried deep within every one of us. It shapes decisions and behaviors until it gets unpacked and sorted through. Unfortunately, for most people, the imprints of youth are left buried and unexplored, as they were in my case for much of my life. It's a mistake to discount your own experiences or compare them to those of others, including mine. Childhood wounds and trauma can take many different forms. People are often reluctant to apply the word "trauma" unless it stems from something universally recognized to be a horrific event or circumstance. I definitely used to feel this way because I'm fully aware that, on the surface, everything I experienced is fairly pedestrian and pales in comparison to the deep hurt inflicted on countless others. But that doesn't make what I experienced any less real or diminish its effect on me. The same principle applies for everyone. Trauma is a personal thing. It can result from something that is present or something that is missing. For example, not being seen or heard can sometimes cause deeper wounds than being physically struck. All that matters is our own reality and how we feel about what we've experienced.

> "No one survives childhood unscathed.
> No parent raises a child without fumbling."
> —*Jedidiah Jenkins*

Through deliberate reflection and self-inquiry, we can begin to develop the level of understanding of ourselves necessary to heal and be at peace. And reaching this higher level of awareness is arguably the single biggest step anyone can take to heal childhood wounds and break cycles. Understanding the source of emotions and behaviors diminishes the power they hold over us. Such self-exploration can be facilitated through activities such as journaling, reading, and deep discussions with those closest to you. But while there is certainly progress to be made on your own and there are many other activities that can be educational and therapeutic, a trained professional can play an invaluable role in seeing things from new perspectives, identifying core issues, facilitating deep work, and finding a path forward. It's like getting a map and navigation tools for your inner world. Unfortunately, in some environments and among certain people there can be a stigma around counseling and therapy. But such attitudes are usually rooted in fear. They are an attempt to avoid discomfort and fail to weigh the prospective value of enlisting support in pursuit of mental health, happiness, and growth.

WHAT DO I WANT FOR YOU?

I want you to know with certainty that, just like me, you were affected by experiences in your childhood, in ways that you may or may not yet be aware of. Experiences that may be hindering your own ability to grow and be happy.

I want you to make it a priority to explore your early days, including the environment, the people (including me), and the experiences that shaped you, and I want you to approach that exploration with curiosity and an open heart.

I want you to experience the cathartic benefits of getting to know yourself on a deeper level and healing childhood wounds. While undertaking such a journey is difficult, it is arguably the single best investment you could make in your personal growth.

I want you to break free of any constraints that may be holding you back so that you can be your authentic self and live your best life.

2

BREAK THE RULES

Individuality, Change, and Taking Control of Your Destiny

> Here's to the crazy ones. The misfits. The rebels. The troublemakers. The round pegs in the square holes. The ones who see things differently. They're not fond of rules. And they have no respect for the status quo. You can quote them, disagree with them, glorify or vilify them. About the only thing you can't do is ignore them. Because they change things. They push the human race forward. And while some may see them as the crazy ones, we see genius. Because the people who are crazy enough to think they can change the world, are the ones who do.
> —*Apple's 1997 Think Different campaign*

> Life is either a daring adventure or nothing. To keep our faces toward change and behave like free spirits in the presence of fate is strength undefeatable.
> —*Helen Keller*

"So let me make sure I understand," I said. "Before you can approve an invoice and process the payment, you need to confirm that the company isn't on that list?"

"That's correct," Bob responded. Bob was an accountant who had worked in the same government office for over twenty years. He handed me the dog-eared, fifteen-page document that was riddled with notations and highlighting. "Each of these vendors has some kind of issue that has made them ineligible for payment. I always highlight the ones that show up most often," he explained. "That way I don't miss them," he added with a hint of pride.

It was 1998, and I was twenty-nine years old, fresh out of business school and working for a large management consulting company. My current assignment was to complete a business process re-engineering study for an accounting office within the Department of Defense. The project involved conducting employee interviews and mapping out the workflow so that we could identify ways to make the operation run more efficiently.

After quickly fanning through the numerous pages of the list Bob had handed me, I asked him the same question I'd already asked a dozen of his colleagues: "Is this list in any particular order?"

"Well, not really," he responded hesitantly. "I mean, I guess maybe it's in order of when the vendors were put on the list? New vendors get added to the bottom before they give us updated copies, and sometimes old ones get removed."

"It seems tedious to have to look through the entire list each time you process a payment," I said. "Do you think there might be an easier way to do this?"

"I don't know. I've never really thought about it," said Bob. "Maybe. But I've been here for a long time and this is how it's always been done, so I'm sure there's a good reason. Of course, back when I first started, the list only had a few dozen companies on it, so it was a lot easier," he said with a hint of wistfulness. "It's gotten a lot longer since then."

After making a few notes, I thanked Bob and excused myself, stepping back into the aisle behind his cubicle. I took a moment to gaze around the cavernous, windowless room that housed the payment operation. Under the glare of large fluorescent overhead lights, I could see hundreds of government accountants just like Bob, hunched over in their respective cubicles, busily processing payments, some of them flipping pages, scanning their copies of the list. By that point I had mapped out the process they were following, timing each step. More than 30 percent of the hours were being spent scanning the same list, line by line, page by page, all day long.

When the study was complete, the final report included a host of recommendations rank-ordered according to which ones would yield the greatest efficiencies at the lowest cost. Unbelievably, the number one recommendation was to make the list easier to search by sorting it alphabetically. And to eventually incorporate a function into the payment software that would flag banned vendors automatically, thereby eliminating the need for the list altogether (the second most impactful recommendation was to remove video games from all the office computers).

It was mind-boggling to me that such an inefficient, senseless process had persisted for decades. I had interviewed dozens of people and, when prompted for an explanation, they revealed a universal hesitancy to question authority or challenge the status quo, combined with blind faith that things must be the way they were for a good reason, which in this instance was certainly not the case. But the most frequent response I received was one that I'd heard so many times before, and it always makes me cringe: "Because that's how we've always done it."

Two decades later I'd find myself in Hawaii, helping to launch a company that took the exact opposite approach.

As I floated on my surfboard, I could hardly believe I wasn't dreaming. I felt the warm breezes as they danced across the ocean and marveled at how the sunshine sparkled on the water's surface like diamonds. I had always wanted to surf, and here I was in Maui at age fifty, getting lessons and catching waves for the first time. It was hard to believe that just a few days earlier I had been back home in northern New York, where I had grown my real estate company for over a decade.

BREAK THE RULES

Despite the success of my company, I felt like I was in a rut, and I'd started planning a new real estate venture. But a timely invitation from my friend Brandon Turner to join him and a small group of other investors for an event in Hawaii would change everything.

As my surfboard bobbed, I breathed in the smells of the ocean and tasted the salt water on my lips. I looked over at Brandon, whose long, red beard was swaying side to side in concert with his arms as he paddled in my direction. The prior day, while traveling with Brandon and his best friend Ryan Murdock on windy roads through Kihei in the back of Ryan's dilapidated minivan, Brandon and I had finalized a plan. Instead of doing my own thing, I agreed to partner with Brandon and Ryan to help them build Open Door Capital, a real estate private equity firm they were in the midst of launching. I felt inspired by Brandon's vision to create a company that was unlike any others in the space, and I knew I would enjoy working with Ryan, who I had gotten to know on the trip. I was nervous about partnering, but I really liked these guys, and I knew from experience that going it alone could be a lonely journey. This was the change I needed, I told myself. Despite my fears, it felt right.

As Brandon pulled up on his board, his face lit up and he flashed a broad smile. In that moment, any lingering doubts receded, and I knew with certainty that I had picked the right business partners. That together we could break new ground and do great things. "We're gonna crush it," I said as our boards rose and dropped in unison with the waves.

"Yeah we are," he replied. The future felt as bright as the Maui sun.

The surfing experience was a special moment for me, not just because it was on my bucket list, but because it was almost prophetic, both in terms of the change for me personally and how Open Door Capital as a company would be different in every way, not only from anything any of us had experienced before, but from the way things were normally done. Working from Brandon's vision, we set some lofty financial goals but refused to accept the hefty tolls that the business world invariably extracts from those who want to achieve such levels of success. Brandon, Ryan, and I had already had our fill of dysfunctional work environments and burnout cultures, and we were determined to leverage our knowledge and experience to avoid the toxic aspects of the corporate world. To do things differently. Instead of working ourselves into an early grave, we would create a workplace that was meaningful, collaborative, and even fun. A startup where people worked hard, but life outside of work mattered and everyone could win.

The launch of Open Door Capital and the government consulting project I had worked on two decades earlier stand out in my mind in stark contrast when it comes to either accepting things as they are or being willing to challenge them. Whether to follow senseless processes, conventions, and rules, or to break them and forge a new and better path. To do what you think is right, regardless of whether it's uncomfortable or unconventional. To be an agent of change.

> "Any fool can make a rule, and any fool will mind it."
> —*Henry David Thoreau*

What followed at Open Door Capital was magical and serves as an example of what can be achieved by doing things your own way. We established a strong set of core values that reflected our goals for the company. We lived by them and hired great people who shared them. We defied convention in many ways, including allowing employees to work remotely (pre-COVID) and having highly flexible work schedules. We hired entrepreneurial people, empowered them, and gave them almost complete autonomy. We created a culture of both extreme ownership and extreme collaboration, and people thrived. When our growth exploded beyond expectations, we declined to bring in seasoned veterans and instead filled positions internally. One of our first part-time interns, Walker Meadows, would eventually advance all the way to COO. After four years, we had nearly a billion dollars in assets under management, led by a talented executive team that was 100 percent promoted from within.

Perhaps more importantly, we mostly evaded the extreme frenetic work and crushing stress that seems practically preordained for hard-charging entrepreneurs. That's not to say we weren't all tested at times, especially in the first couple of years, but we also had fun and created a lot of great memories. Some of the experiences that I shared with my cofounders and executive team include things like a mountain-bike ride down the side of a volcano, whale watching on paddle boards, a company sand-sculpting competition, trips to Las Vegas where we saw shows and UFC fights, and a kayaking excursion through the alligator-infested swamps of Louisiana.

We accomplished everything we set out to do, and so much more. Led by Brandon, who constantly challenges convention and refuses to accept that anything is impossible, we did things our own way and found creative solutions to countless problems. For example, in the summer of 2022 we found ourselves unable to raise enough capital to complete the purchase of several large investment properties we had under contract. This is not something we had experienced before, but with the stock market cratering and interest rates skyrocketing, many of our investors were paralyzed with fear. I thought we'd need to pull the plug on the deals and lose millions of dollars in non-refundable deposits, but Brandon was undeterred. He believed we could overcome the obstacle by launching an innovative social media marketing campaign, and that's what we did. In order to help execute the plan and field all the new investor calls, a host of new processes were created on the fly, and employees volunteered to pitch in from all levels and divisions of the company. We had taken a leap of faith and jumped out of the plane, and the company rallied to build parachutes on the way down. The result was nothing short of astonishing. We not only raised the capital to close the deals in a challenging environment, but we doubled the size of our investor base. It was a testament to the company culture we had built and a truly extraordinary thing to witness and be a part of. One of the greatest lessons I learned from this experience and others like it is how powerful it can be to free yourself of the assumptions and constraints imposed by the world around you. To never just do things because that's how they've always been done. If you can break out of the box, innovate, and forge your own path, anything is possible.

> "Be daring, be different, be impractical, be anything that will assert integrity of purpose and imaginative vision against the play-it-safers, the creatures of the commonplace, the slaves of the ordinary."
> —*Cecil Beaton*

These examples are based on business practices, but the same principle applies in all areas of life, including your own personal decisions, big and small. We live in a world that is rife with regulations, traditions, conventions, and beliefs that are sometimes as illogical as they are inflexible. From an early age, we find that boundaries and lanes are defined, and we're expected to stay within them. Rules are set, both explicit and unspoken, that we're expected to follow, often on blind faith or from a place of fear. And while some of these rules are reasonable, many are not. Yet too few people are willing to challenge established things that don't make sense, don't seem right, or aren't in alignment with who they are as individuals. Instead, they meekly conform to the people and environment around them, sometimes at the expense of their integrity or sense of self.

Unfortunately, there is an unsettling tendency for all of us to end up on a trajectory that we steadily move along, taking the path of least resistance, following rules, and taking the actions that others expect of us. The tendency is to let ourselves float along with the momentum, like a tube ride on a lazy river. We go where it takes us. Until we are no longer thinking for ourselves. We're no longer growing. We're just along for the ride, going round and round wherever that lazy river takes us, leaving our destiny to outside forces.

> "The fault, dear Brutus, is not in our stars, but in ourselves."
> —*William Shakespeare*

I'm proud of those times in my life when I was self-aware enough to recognize that I wasn't happy or something didn't feel right, and I mustered up the courage to make changes. This was the case when I decided to join Open Door Capital. It didn't matter that my company was successful at the time, or that the easiest, safest, and arguably most responsible decision would be to stay exactly where I was. The truth is I felt adrift and was no longer finding fulfillment in my job. The systems and team were in place, and things could run without me. My learning curve had flattened, and I didn't feel challenged anymore. The problem with these kinds of situations is that, as Chinese philosopher Lao Tzu wrote, "If you do not change direction, you might end up where you are heading." If I kept doing the same thing, I would be bored and miserable.

I felt the same way in my first job after college when, after working as an engineer for five years, I made the difficult decision to quit and join the Peace Corps. People questioned the wisdom of this decision, and I felt the weight of their judgment and opinions, all the more so because their viewpoints seemed sensible. But it was time to make a change and do something else, even if it meant a loss of income or seemed illogical to others. Sometimes, in the words of St. Thérèse of Lisieux, "there is no merit in doing what reason dictates." This was one of those times. While difficult to quantify, what my decision brought was a spark of hope. The potential to walk an alternative path that would provide deeper fulfillment. To do something that would enrich my life more than crunching numbers in a cubicle.

> "Growth is painful. Change is painful. But nothing is as painful as staying stuck somewhere you don't belong."
> —*N. R. Narayana Murthy*

Unfortunately, setting a new course is rarely simple. Because change is hard. Being different is hard. It's unsettling. It's scary. But it's also necessary for growth, and sometimes for your own well-being. It's necessary if you want to control your own fate and lead a full life. So how do you do it? As with most other areas of growth, it starts with awareness. Being conscious of all the pressures and influences around you and within you that are trying to make you conform. And then you need to take deliberate action. To trust in yourself and bravely do what best serves you, not what's expected by society, coworkers, family, friends, or anyone else. To have the courage to be different or even disliked. To be a wolf and not a sheep. Wolves are free spirits that rely heavily on their intelligence and instinct to guide them. They are naturally friendly, curious, and playful, but, when necessary, they can be strong and fierce. They certainly don't allow themselves to be influenced by expectations or care what anyone thinks about them. We would all be better off if we were a little less preoccupied, a little more untamed, and trusted our hearts and souls to do what felt right. Taking control of our own lives instead of making fear-based decisions or leaving our destiny in the hands of others.

> "The most difficult thing is the decision to act. The rest is merely tenacity. The fears are paper tigers. You can do anything you decide to do. You can act to change and control your life."
> —*Amelia Earhart*

While being an agent of change has the potential to be personally and professionally transformational, that doesn't mean that you should abandon sound judgment, particularly with regards to where you direct your efforts. There is an important balance to be struck here. Experience has taught me to focus my energy and efforts on those things that *can* be changed or controlled, and hold space for accepting those things that cannot—principles embodied in the Serenity Prayer and widely popularized by Alcoholics Anonymous. Nothing has caused me more angst and been less productive than fretting over things I have no control over. Engaging in such concerns is not only futile, but it's wasted energy. Like having a leak in the gas tank of your car, draining fuel that could take you in the direction you want to go. And yet it's something that most of us do incessantly. Learning to just let these things go has helped bring me peace of mind and allowed me to dedicate myself more fully to the things I actually can influence.

The key is to be sure you're accepting and letting go of the right things. Arguably the most critical but less appreciated aspect of the Serenity Prayer is invoked in the last line—having the wisdom to accurately distinguish between what is within your control and what is not. For most people, there is a strong natural tendency to lump most of life into the category of things that cannot be changed because it's easier to rationalize not trying to do things that are uncomfortable or difficult in the short term. Or attempting something that, while possible, has a high probability of failure. The truth is that it's often worth taking a shot at something because *sometimes good things happen.* You have far more power to influence things than you realize. To manifest your destiny in ways that may seem improbable. Recognizing this, and having the courage to change the things you can, will change your life.

> "God, grant me the serenity
> to accept the things I cannot change,
> the courage to change the things I can,
> and the wisdom to know the difference."
> —*Serenity Prayer*

WHAT DO I WANT FOR YOU?

I want you to recognize all the internal and external forces trying to resist change and keep you in your lane. I want you to see that the world is filled with rules and conventions, both stated and implied, and to know that they don't all make sense and, in some cases, may even be harmful.

I want you to question things and make up your own mind about what's right and what's possible. To find the will to resist the forces that would stifle you and to take action.

I want you to embrace some of the spirit embodied in the opening quote of this chapter—to be a misfit, a rebel, a troublemaker. To be a round peg in a square hole. To be one who sees things differently, is not fond of rules, and has no respect for the status quo.

I want you to change things. To break rules. To push things forward. To be free. To do things your own way, take control of your destiny, and live life on your own terms.

3

MINDSET

Conquering Limiting Beliefs and Unleashing Potential

> If you think small, your world will be small.
> If you think big, your world will be big.
> —*Paulo Coelho*

> Don't limit yourself. Many people limit themselves to what they think they can do. You can go as far as your mind lets you. What you believe, remember, you can achieve.
> —*Mary Kay Ash*

As I approached the steep hill to the finish line, I felt intense pain throughout my body, but especially in my legs. My quads felt like there were daggers stuck in them, and it took a concerted effort to stay upright and move in the right direction, let alone run. I was nearing the end of my first ultramarathon, a fifty kilometer (thirty-one mile) trail race through Smith Rock State Park near Bend, Oregon. The scenery was so beautiful that it seemed like something out of a storybook, but in that moment, I wasn't able to enjoy the views because I was too consumed by my suffering and the large hill looming just ahead. That final long, steep climb was all that stood between me and the finish line.

My journey to Smith Rock was an improbable one. It had started about four months earlier when, at age fifty-one, I applied to participate in season nine of *Becoming Ultra*, a program that supports and chronicles amateur athletes training for their first ultramarathon. Participants are matched with a coach and asked to share their experience on social media and the *Becoming Ultra* podcast. Applying to the program required a fair amount of faith and courage because I had serious doubts about whether I could successfully complete the training for an ultra, let alone finish the race itself. I had only recently recovered from a debilitating back injury that had sidelined me for more than a year, and trail running was new to me. While I had quickly grown to love my forays into the woods, I still took frequent spills as I adjusted to navigating uneven trails littered with roots and rocks. My prior running had been on relatively flat, smooth pavement, whereas completing an ultramarathon would require me to run farther than I'd ever run before, and do so on mountainous terrain, which was a daunting proposition.

Listening to the selection show on the *Becoming Ultra* podcast, I was surprised to hear that I'd been chosen to participate in the program, and I felt a surge of panic. Not only had I committed to do something I didn't think I was physically capable of, but I had agreed to chronicle the entire fiasco on social media and podcast appearances. But the positive news, which I didn't fully appreciate yet, was that I had been paired with a coach, Ian Sharman, who would prove to be extremely knowledgeable, drawing from both his extensive coaching experience and his highly distinguished career as a professional ultrarunner. Ian's personality was also a perfect fit for me—he's very candid, yet also tactful, which is a rare combination that I appreciated. And he didn't hesitate to challenge me.

What ensued were months of training that tested me incessantly and defied my logic. Ian would assign me workouts that I would almost always balk at. "Doesn't he know how old I am," I'd ask myself. "I can't do that. I know myself. I'm just going to get injured." But when I tentatively expressed my doubts to Ian, he always provided the perfect blend of encouragement and logic. "I think you can do it," he'd say. "Give it a try. If you don't feel like you can run the full distance, then you can just power hike the rest of it." Other times, he'd send me an article or podcast addressing specific concerns. But he never let me off the hook just because I was afraid or skeptical. So I'd head out on these seemingly crazy long runs, cursing Ian, entirely convinced I couldn't do it, but too embarrassed not to try. Once I started, though, I'd keep putting one foot in front of the other and, somehow, I'd invariably manage to get the run done. And the same scenario played out again and again as my training progressed. For months. I'd get assigned a workout. I'd go out to do the run, completely convinced Ian was pushing me too hard and I couldn't do it. And then I'd do it. And I'd be surprised. Every. Single. Time. Shockingly, I trained for three months without missing a single day, despite frequent travel and some trying conditions, running through storms, floods, and all kinds of dubious situations. With Ian pushing me to new heights and my own steadfast determination to try my best, the progress became more difficult to deny, and my mindset shifted. Instead of feeling surprised, I began to feel encouraged. And I slowly developed a belief in myself. That I could do it. That I could run an ultramarathon.

When race day finally arrived, I felt more ready and confident than I would have thought possible. I was proud of what I had achieved over the course of my training, and I viewed the race as a chance to celebrate that accomplishment. I also got the nicest surprise. A group of friends showed up on race morning. They had followed my journey on social media and traveled from all across the country to support me on race day, some from as far away as Hawaii. They even had shirts made to show their support. To be on the receiving end of this gesture was deeply moving and something I will always be grateful for.

The race itself proved even more demanding than I had feared. But my friends found places along the course to cheer me on, providing a huge lift. And now, as I approached the end, I was at the very limit of my endurance. I could see the final climb ahead, and it was so steep that it seemed like a cruel joke. I imagined the heartless race director laying out the course route, laughing sadistically about the last half mile and the pain it would inflict. I knew there was no way I could possibly run up such a hill at this point, so I prepared to hike it. And then, seemingly out of nowhere, some of my friends appeared yet again, shouting encouragement and running alongside me. With their support, I was able to prove myself wrong one more time. With my friend Ashley shouting at me like a drill sergeant, and other friends in tow offering their support, I somehow mustered reserves I didn't know I had and doggedly ran all the way up the final hill. I crossed the finish line and collapsed, completely spent. But as I lay on the ground in pain, looking up at the bright blue sky, I smiled and felt a deep sense of fulfillment. A fulfillment derived both from the kindness of my friends and from the act of challenging myself. I had tested my limits of endurance and done something that I hadn't believed I could possibly do. I was now an ultrarunner.

After successfully completing my first ultramarathon, I had a new respect for what my body could do. Given how challenging the race was, I didn't expect I could run farther than I did on that beautiful day in Smith Rock State Park. But then again, I now knew that my internal barometer wasn't necessarily an accurate gauge. So I decided to keep going. The following year I'd run a fifty-mile race. And despite believing yet again that I'd reached my limit, the year after that, in the midst of writing this book, I completed the Black Canyon 100K (sixty-two miles). It took me over sixteen hours to finish, but I covered *double* the distance of that first ultra in Smith Rock. If that weren't enough, I ran the last fifteen miles with a large cactus thorn so deeply embedded in my toe that it would later require surgery to remove it.

How far can I possibly go? And what other things am I capable of? The only thing I can say for sure is that it's probably more than I believe. And I'll never know unless I try.

Have you ever thought about doing something hard and let the belief that you're not capable stop you or slow you down? I learned many things from my ultrarunning journey, but the most important takeaway is that we're all capable of doing so much more than we think we can do. *You* are capable of far more than you can imagine. I had already reached this conclusion in the context of business. But for some reason I had never internalized the lesson deeply enough to apply it to other areas of my life. In the case of my first ultramarathon, I felt like my abilities were limited by a combination of factors, but especially age, prior injuries, and genetics. The truth is that, like most people, I was far more hemmed in by my own mental barriers than I was by any physical constraints. And I didn't even realize it.

> "The only impossible journey is the one you never begin."
> —*Tony Robbins*

I'm certainly not alone in having limiting beliefs. We all create mental frameworks around our abilities, and sadly we have a strong tendency to underestimate ourselves. Our self-perceptions are influenced by the thoughts in our heads that arise from a deeply ingrained predisposition to reject anything that poses a threat, whether real or perceived. Basically, we're hardwired to stay safe. And not just physically safe. Safe from failure or rejection. Safe from the scrutiny, opinions, and judgment of others. Safe from the hard work and sacrifices that might be involved. Safe from whatever other fears we hold. Such instincts can be valuable and have their place, but they don't always serve us well, especially when we have big aspirations or want to realize our full potential. Left unchecked, our fears will manifest as voices in our heads telling us all the reasons why we're overreaching or incapable. Why something isn't possible, or isn't worth trying. So we think to ourselves: "No. I can't do it." Because it's a whole lot easier and safer to convince ourselves that something isn't possible than it is to put ourselves out there and take the risk of trying.

> "If we all did the things we are capable of doing
> we would literally astound ourselves."
> —*Thomas Edison*

Our base instincts and the incessant chatter in our heads make any change in mindset around what we're capable of very difficult, particularly when we try to approach that change head-on with logic. And pronouncements to ourselves in the mirror like "I'm capable of anything I set my mind to" tend to fall flat. What's worked better for me is to take a more indirect approach. First, I have adopted a belief that anything worthwhile is worth trying, and failure is an acceptable price to pay in exchange for a chance to do something meaningful. I allow myself to consider all the possible outcomes of any endeavor, and rarely are the downsides as severe under objective scrutiny as they are in the dramatic and sinister recesses of our minds. Knowing that I can survive the consequences of an undesirable outcome diffuses the root fear that would otherwise derail my aspirations before I ever get started. If I had let my anxieties and limiting beliefs curtail me, I would never have done any of the things that have brought me the most fulfillment in life. That's not to say everything always works out, because it doesn't. I've failed and made mistakes more times than I can count. But those experiences also helped me realize that setbacks are valuable because they're essential to personal expansion—it's how we learn, and how we grow. It provides the seeds from which a garden of wisdom can emerge. And it makes us stronger. It frees us from the shackles of our anxieties. Every time I fail at something, I pick myself back up, life goes on, and fear loses a little more of its grip on me moving forward.

> "Everything you want is on the other side of fear."
> —*Jack Canfield*

Another lesson I've learned is never to look at a big goal as a single step. Because that step is invariably too big and intimidating to wrap your head around—more like a deep, dark, gaping chasm. Instead of thinking, "I'm incapable," ask yourself, "What is a small step I can take right now to help me get just a little bit closer to my goal?" As Martin Luther King Jr. said, "You don't have to see the whole staircase, just take the first step." It might just be doing a little research online, making a phone call, or reading the next chapter of a book. All big goals need to be broken down into many, many, small, manageable bites. Instead of trying to leap across the chasm, you figure out how to build yourself a bridge, piece by piece. And then comes the really hard part—*taking action*. Mark Twain said, "The secret of getting ahead is getting started. The secret of getting started is breaking your complex overwhelming tasks into small manageable tasks, and starting on the first one." And don't wait to be inspired before you take that first step. As author Mark Manson posited in his book *The Subtle Art of Not Giving a F*ck*, motivation follows action, not the other way around. Just take those feet that are stuck in the mud, pull them out, and start walking in the direction you want to go.

Once underway, you're the beneficiary of Newton's first law—it takes a lot less energy to propel a body already in motion than to move an object at rest. The second step, third step, fourth step, and so on come easier as momentum builds and carries you forward with less effort. It evolves into a routine that becomes a habit. Confidence builds, and progress is made. The power of taking small steps consistently over time is mind boggling. If you spend even fifteen to thirty minutes a day working toward something for a few years, you can accomplish more extraordinary things than you could possibly imagine. It doesn't matter if it's learning Italian, starting a business, practicing meditation, or playing pickleball. I can promise you that you'll achieve more than you think.

> "A pagoda of nine stories is built from small bricks."
> —*Lao Tzu*

The last lesson I've learned related to mindset and doing things that stretch you is that you don't need to do it alone. Enlisting others in my journey has provided benefits such as motivation, guidance, support, companionship, and accountability. It can also help you address underlying fears and overcome legitimate limitations, which improves the likelihood of a successful outcome.

Be willing to fail. Go step by step. Stick with it. Get support from others more knowledgeable and experienced than you.

This is the blueprint for how I completed my ultramarathon, but it's also a strategy that has served me well in many different endeavors. It's a recipe for success that can be applied to all areas of life. The positive outcomes have allowed me to fully adopt the mindset that I am capable of doing more than those pesky voices in my head might otherwise lead me to believe. And so are you.

> "You are braver than you believe, stronger than you seem,
> and smarter than you think."
> —*Christopher Robin*

WHAT DO I WANT FOR YOU?

I want you to know that, just like me, you're capable of doing far more than you think you can, in all areas of life. That any obstacle is surmountable. That any limits are self-imposed, and that your beliefs about what's possible are not an accurate gauge of your abilities. Your self-assessment of what you're capable of lags reality by a wide margin.

I want you to be aware of the voice in your head telling you what you can and cannot do, and recognize that it arises from a primitive compulsion to keep you safe, physically and emotionally. And I want you to be strong enough to rise above it. To objectively assess the risk of failure and not be afraid to have big goals. To be willing to make mistakes and to learn and grow from them.

I want you to embrace a growth mindset and not shy away from having big dreams. To see large challenges as a culmination of many small, manageable steps. When something is important to you, I want you to focus on identifying and taking the first small step in the direction you want to go. To get started and then have the determination to propel yourself forward. To harness the power that comes from taking consistent steps toward a meaningful endeavor over a long period of time.

I want you to be humble enough and courageous enough to ask for help when it makes sense. To strategically enlist the aid of others as you pursue your goals.

I want you to rise above your limiting beliefs and make your dreams a reality.

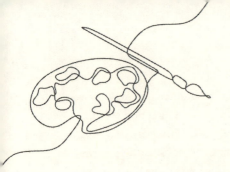

4

CREATE

Experiencing the Magic of Being a Creator

> Creative work is not a selfish act or a bid for attention on the part of the actor. It's a gift to the world and every being in it. Don't cheat us of your contribution. Give us what you've got.
> —*Steven Pressfield*

> An artist cannot fail; it is a success to be one.
> —*Charles Horton Cooley*

I glanced around at the nearby tables and booths in Panera to check that we had enough privacy, then looked across the table to make sure I had my wife's full attention. I was anxious, but also excited, so I decided to go ahead and jump right in.

"Okay, so you know I've been spending a lot of time working on my real estate book," I began. "Well, my agent sent the book proposal to every publisher he could think of that might be a good fit, and everyone has said no. But he likes my writing and thinks there's something there. So he's encouraging me to self-publish," I said. "He referred me to a great editor who is willing to help me through the process. But unfortunately, if I take this route and do it the right way, it's not going to be cheap," I said.

"What will it cost?" she asked. "And what are your hopes?"

"Well..." I hesitated, uncomfortable to share what I really thought. But I knew it was best to be completely transparent. "I think the all-in cost to self-publish in a way that I can be proud of will probably be between $10,000 and $15,000," I said. "And to be honest, without the support of a publisher, I don't expect to ever sell enough copies of the book to recover that. I would say the best-case scenario would be that someday, maybe five to ten years from now, if the book is wildly successful, I could break even. But I think we have to assume we'll never get that money back," I added. "I'm basing this on my prior experience. Do you remember the other book I told you about that I authored a long time ago? It did terrible, and that book had the support of a major publisher. I got a $5,000 advance and it never even sold enough for me to see another dime. I did the math one time and figured out that I made less than $2 per hour for all the time I put into it."

I could see that my pitch wasn't going very well, so I shared the rest of what was on my mind. "Listen, I know this is a lot of money, and it's going to consume a ton of my time, but it's really important to me. Now that I've had success in real estate and achieved some level of notoriety, I get so many people asking me for mentorship or advice. They want to do what I've done, and I want to help them. I can't mentor everyone, but I feel compelled to share what I've learned. The mistakes I've made. People need to know they can do it if they want to. And if I can capture it all in this book, every time someone is looking for help, I can just give them a copy. I also think I can create something that's different from anything else out there—a real estate book that has stories and humor. Something that's engaging. But mostly it's just a way I can give back and help people. It's something I really want to do, and I wanted to see what you thought."

To her credit, she didn't hesitate. "I think you should do it," she responded matter-of-factly. I felt an immediate surge of relief. "I understand it's not about the money, and we can afford it anyway," she said. "If it's important to you, then I support it 100 percent."

The book that I eventually authored and self-published as a result of this conversation was *Crushing It in Apartments and Commercial Real Estate*, which went viral shortly after publication and would go on to sell more than a hundred thousand copies, which (to the best of my knowledge) makes it the bestselling self-published real estate book of all time. I recognize that this is a somewhat middling distinction, and I certainly don't consider myself an acclaimed author by any stretch, but I take pride in my creation and the fact that it resonated with so many readers.

Why did *Crushing It in Apartments and Commercial Real Estate* do so well? I think there are a variety of reasons, but perhaps the biggest is the purity of the motivations behind it. A genuine desire to create something of substance that might make a positive difference. And the freedom to express myself in a way that was unique and genuine. I felt like I had something inside of me that needed to come out, and I had the capacity to create it. The hard work involved was a labor of love. All of which made the project meaningful and personally fulfilling in a way that any artist or creator can understand.

> "If I create from the heart, nearly everything works;
> if from the head, almost nothing."
> —Marc Chagall

The entire experience stands in stark contrast to that of the first book I authored, which I'm embarrassed to say was ego-driven and motivated by all the wrong reasons. I wanted to impress others and establish credibility within my field. I sought media attention and speaking invitations. I dreamed of selling a lot of copies and making money. Maybe landing a better job or future book deals. In the end, while I think that book was well written, the delusions of grandeur and selfish motivations resulted in a work product that was shallow and didn't resonate with myself or the reader. Even if the publisher had somehow managed to sell more copies, the book didn't come from a good place and would never be something I could take real pride in. I got exactly what I deserved, which happened to be less than two dollars per hour. It would have been more profitable to spend that time at a minimum wage job, though I can now appreciate the value of the lessons learned from my hubris.

Steven Pressfield captures the essence of this sentiment in his classic *The War of Art* when he says, "We must do our work for its own sake, not for fortune or attention or applause." More pointedly, he also states that "to labor in the arts for any reason other than love is prostitution." While such an assertion could be considered harsh, and I don't particularly love the characterization of my initial foray into the literary world as an act of prostitution, I believe his statement has merit.

Pressfield's *The War of Art* does an exceptional job of examining the resistance and challenges we all face when we create, provides a healthy dose of motivation, and explains why creation is such a noble endeavor—perhaps even an imperative. Pressfield also delves into the spiritual aspects of creation and encourages us to stay pure in our motivations and harness our unique gifts to create for a higher purpose. To view ourselves as conduits through which God can bring something wonderful into the universe, for its own sake and not to satiate our egos.

The most beautiful man-made things that have existed in the world were created for the sake of expression and without the weight of expectations. They certainly weren't done for the purpose of generating wealth or adulation. And it is perhaps the greatest irony of art and other creative endeavors that these works are the ones that tend to bring the greatest spiritual and material rewards for both the creator and anyone who bears witness. Nobel Peace Prize laureate Malala Yousafzai calls art "a way of making the world a better place, of creating beauty and meaning." But even when creations don't achieve wide acclaim, are by all accounts ordinary, or are never shared with another person, there are intrinsic benefits to the work that goes into the creation process that can allow us to be more present and generate feelings of peace and fulfillment. Creation is food for the soul. It waters our gardens within. And the capacity to create in this manner and realize such benefits lies in each of us; it's just more latent in some than others. Pablo Picasso made the same observation when he said that "every child is an artist; the problem is staying an artist when you grow up." If you can set your ego aside, you can awaken that childhood creator that lies dormant and reap the rewards.

Studies have shown that engaging in creative acts can also yield a host of health benefits, providing relaxation and improving mental health. Creative expression can be a platform for self-inquiry and help foster positivity. Brené Brown calls art "a form of therapy, a way of working through your thoughts and feelings." I think anyone who has immersed themselves in a creative project has experienced this to one degree or another and can attest to the positive mental aspects. In addition, acts of creation can help build relationships and foster community. Oprah Winfrey characterized art as "a way of connecting with others, of sharing your story and your experiences." Meanwhile, arts that involve movement, such as dance or playing a musical instrument, can also improve physical fitness levels, yielding a host of additional health rewards. Each form of creative endeavor brings its own array of unique benefits.

> "Practicing an art, no matter how well or badly, is a way to make your soul grow, for heaven's sake. Sing in the shower. Dance to the radio. Tell stories. Write a poem to a friend, even a lousy poem. Do it as well as you possibly can. You will get an enormous reward. You will have created something."
> —*Kurt Vonnegut*

If you'd like to experience the advantages of creativity but aren't sure how to approach it, Rick Rubin's book *The Creative Act: A Way of Being* is a great resource. An accomplished music industry executive and record producer, Rubin has worked with acts such as the Beastie Boys, Metallica, Red Hot Chili Peppers, Johnny Cash, and Aerosmith, among many others. In *The Creative Act*, Rubin delves into seventy-eight "areas of thought" that will help you maximize creativity and produce the finest works of art that you're capable of. Rubin calls creativity "a fundamental aspect of humanity" and, like Steven Pressfield, he takes a spiritual view of creation, suggesting that creative acts are born from something beyond ourselves, which he calls Source.

Rubin also explains that "to create is to bring something into existence that wasn't there before," and that "creativity doesn't exclusively relate to making art." I agree with these observations; it's important to avoid placing rigid boundaries on what we consider acts of creation—to forgo judgement and define it in the broadest and most accepting terms. The core principles of being a creator extend into many different areas of life, including the establishment and growth of businesses and nonprofits. The motivations behind entrepreneurial pursuits are just as important as those for writing, painting, or sculpture. In my experience, the purity of intent and commitment to any organization's purpose, values, and culture have proven to be fundamental to its success and the ultimate contribution it stands to make, both in the lives of its staff and patrons and to the world as a whole. Such things are real, and they make all the difference. Because in the end, whether we're talking about an organization or an individual, if a creation is born from a good place with pure intentions, the forces of the universe always seem to marshal themselves and align in its favor.

WHAT DO I WANT FOR YOU?

I want you to make it a priority to create. To have an appreciation for the value and sanctity of the creation process and to bring new things to life that are born of pure intentions. Most people are confined within a mental framework that is bounded by what already exists. I want you to free yourself from these constraints and have vision for what might be. To see the voids in the world around you and harness your unique talents to fill them.

I want you to see the beauty and experience the fulfillment that comes from creating things. Whether it's art, an invention, a practice, a computer program, a book, an event, a design, an organization, a course, or a new recipe. Anything and everything. It doesn't matter. Just adopt a creation mindset and experience the magic of being a creator.

I want you to create without judgment. To give yourself grace. Talent can emerge and grow over time, but it isn't a prerequisite for being a creator. Even doing things badly can bring you a taste of the joy and fulfillment that only creators can know.

Finally, I want you to create solely for the sake of personal expression and creation itself, bringing beautiful things into the world. To lift yourself up and do the work with a purity of intention, free of the unhealthy influences of ego. If you can do this, the rewards will come, more so because that's not what you were seeking. But they will come, and your life *will* be that much richer as a result.

5

DELAYED GRATIFICATION

The Power and Perils of Sacrificing for the Future

> The cause of most of man's unhappiness is sacrificing what he wants most for what he wants now.
> —*Gordon B. Hinckley*

> The ability to discipline yourself to delay gratification in the short term in order to enjoy greater rewards in the long term is the indispensable prerequisite for success.
> —*Brian Tracy*

The heavy snow was being whipped around by biting gusts of wind, reducing the glare of the nearby streetlamps to a faint, hazy glow. The roaring wind and snow swallowed up most sounds, but they couldn't fully stifle the angry growl of the thirty-inch snowblower I was maneuvering—its 400cc engine was running at full throttle, and I held on tightly as the machine wildly bucked around. Vibrations reverberated up my arms as the snowblower labored to carve a path through the deep drifts and hurl the snow back out into the fury of the storm. It was another early January morning in Watertown, New

York, where such brutal conditions occur with too much regularity, testing the hardy souls whose circumstances dictate a confrontation with the elements.

I was thirty-nine years old, about seven months into my real estate investing journey, and it wasn't pretty. My first rental property was a large office building that had been severely mismanaged by the prior owners. Other buyers had been deterred, but where they saw distress and neglect, I had seen opportunity. I was convinced that with enough grit and determination, this historic structure could be returned to its former glory. So I cashed in my retirement savings to make this dubious purchase and then rolled up my sleeves, buckled down, and went to work, steadily and determinedly polishing my diamond in the rough. I had made a lot of progress, but it had been a rough road, requiring a lot of sacrifice. At this stage, every dollar mattered, and I was committed to doing as much of the work myself as possible. Unfortunately, this included unpleasant tasks like picking up trash, unclogging toilets, and, on days like today, coming in before dawn to remove snow and ice from the myriad of sidewalks and stairs, spreading salt, and then opening up the building before heading off to my teaching job at the local community college.

The snowblower's light penetrated the darkness enough to illuminate my path, but the bitter cold and furious winds made everything more trying. As I exhaled, the moisture from my breath kept fogging my glasses and freezing my eyelashes together. I ventured a look behind me. Peeking out over the scarf that covered the lower half of my face, squinting from the cold and swirling snow, I was disheartened to see the sidewalk I had just cleared was already filling with freshly fallen snow. The neat sides of my clearly cut path were now misshapen with small drifts created by the howling winds. It was 6:00 a.m., and I'd already been outside for an hour. It crushed my spirit to know with certainty I'd soon need to clear the same areas all over again. The thought was interrupted by shooting pains in my hands and feet. The cold was starting to penetrate my gloves and boots. I paused the snowblower, stamped my feet, and furiously shook my hands, opening and closing them, trying to get the blood to circulate and combat the needles and numbness. Not for the first time, my mind flashed to what I was missing. I could be home in a warm bed right now. Alexa and Jackie would be waking up soon, having breakfast, and getting ready for school—a routine I was no longer a part of. I wouldn't see them until I returned home for dinner that evening. I'd eat with them and help put them to bed. My favorite part of the day was reading them bedtime stories. And then after they went down, I'd pull my computer out and get some more work done. I squeezed my eyes shut and grimaced in anguish. When the emotional pain came, it was worse than any physical discomfort. Sometimes I was tormented by my decisions: plagued with doubts, desperately trying to do what was right, but sometimes just as desperately uncertain what "right" even was.

"Aaaaaggghhhh!" I bellowed at the top of my lungs.

"What the hell am I doing?" I asked myself. I was steadfastly determined to be a good provider and build a better life for myself and my loved ones. But at what price? Was it worth it? These are questions I'd asked myself a thousand times, and over the next decade, I'd ask the same questions a thousand times more.

Part of the reason I started my real estate company was that I wanted to take control of my own destiny and do things the right way: create something I could be proud of and generate wealth on my own terms, without making sacrifices in other areas of my life. I didn't want to repeat the mistakes of my past. In the short term, I hoped my investments would generate some income to help supplement the meager salary I earned as a professor, a position that afforded generous time off, flexibility, and fulfillment—things I greatly appreciated after burning myself out at my last job. The tech company I had worked for suffered from a venomous culture, and I pushed myself over the edge there—a five-year sprint during which I sacrificed practically everything at the altar of work, chasing illusory dreams of stock option riches and notoriety. I remember running into a former business school classmate and bragging that I was routinely putting in hundred-hour work weeks, something which now strikes me as nothing but sad. "Wow," he dutifully responded, "that's *insane*." His characterization was so much more accurate than he could have realized. What did I gain for such herculean efforts? Besides a prodigious increase in my waistline, I was rewarded with a nice, big wrecking ball. A wrecking ball that not only destroyed my physical and mental health but also my relationships. I completely lost touch with friends and family during those years, and I strained a marriage that would eventually end in divorce. And that big pot of gold at the end of the rainbow? That gratification that I had delayed? It never came. Not that it mattered, because no payday would have been worth the price I paid.

"This time," I told myself, "it will be different." But despite my best intentions, building a real estate empire would sometimes test me and those around me. Sacrifices were still made. In addition to the demands on my time, there was a fair amount of stress and financial strain, particularly in the early days. I put my entire life savings on the line to buy my first investment property, so there was a lot at stake, and it soon became clear that ensuring my company's survival and maximizing growth would require reinvesting all the money it generated back into the business. So even though I had started investing to improve my financial situation, I made the difficult decision not to pay myself. Instead, I kept my day job for almost a decade and supported my family primarily with my teaching salary, deferring financial rewards until later. Observing my frugality and dedication to reinvesting profits, a fellow investor labeled me "the king of delayed gratification." By any objective measure, the business results of adopting this approach were astonishing. In less than ten years I achieved financial freedom, and after fifteen years, I had amassed a real estate portfolio of more than ten thousand rental units. While such an outcome may seem glorious in the abstract, the road traveled to get there was riddled with potholes, accidents, and detours.

DELAYED GRATIFICATION

> "All things come to those who wait."
> —*Violet Fane*

Thankfully, my prior experience with overwork wasn't lost on me—so despite a profusion of challenges and mistakes, I also managed to get a lot right. Sacrifices were made, particularly in the early years, but I got much better at things along the way. As my business grew, I was able to pay others to complete some of the more unpleasant tasks, like the snow removal and property maintenance. By outsourcing and delegating, I freed up time that could be reallocated to other activities. I hired people and created systems that could run without me. I also took better care of myself and was present for loved ones. I certainly wasn't perfect, but I was more self-aware and maintained a better balance than I had in the past, eventually creating a life with nearly complete time freedom. In the end, the entire journey, good and bad, provided an incredible education. I learned lessons not only about myself, but about work and business, about life, and about the intersection of those things.

Delayed gratification, or sacrificing what you desire now to achieve your long-term goals, while difficult to do, is an exceptionally powerful practice, and it's one that almost anyone who attains a high level of personal or professional success embraces on one level or another. Does it always work out as intended? Obviously not—it didn't for me at my tech job. But wielded wisely—strategically deferring the right things and embracing the journey toward a meaningful purpose—the potential is practically limitless. Choose any accomplished businessperson, historical figure, professional athlete, artist, or celebrity. Behind every story of greatness there can be found an exceptional level of discipline, hard work, and sacrifice. They didn't get there through indulgence. They were driven. Trade-offs were made. Their resolve was tested. Dues were exacted. Prices were paid. And it was all much messier than it looks from the outside. Was it worth it? Only they can say, though the answer will likely depend on how much fulfillment they derived along the way rather than on any fame or material rewards.

A few years back I was at a conference and heard a motivational speaker talk about what it took to be successful. "Every person who really makes it big has to give up at least a decade of their life, where they do nothing but grind hard in pursuit of their dreams," he said. "They have a singularity of purpose, and everything else takes a back seat. You have to make sacrifices. You have to pay your dues if you want to reap the rewards." There is truth to this statement, but if you're that ambitious and choose to go to that extreme, you also need to make sure that such single-minded focus is appropriately directed and aligned with your best interests. Otherwise, it's like lifting weights every day without proper technique. You're just going to hurt yourself. This is what happened to me. I toiled for years in corporate settings, which helped me climb the ladder and afford nicer things, but it also took a severe personal toll. How do you avoid such a mistake? And if a goal requires such sacrifice, is the juice even worth the squeeze? As with most things in life, it depends. Just because you *can* do something doesn't mean it's a good idea. The devil is in the details. Hopefully the following reflections and advice will provide you some clarity without you having to learn the way I did, through painful mistakes.

Let's start with the fact that at its essence, delayed gratification involves a transaction. You're giving up something now in order to receive something better in return later. People get into trouble when they run forward blindly, sacrificing precious things without a second thought, often for goals that are illusory or misguided. It's far better to live with intention and adopt a more measured approach. To recognize and deliberately evaluate the exchange as you would any other transaction. To assess, in essence, the potential return on investment of your limited resources, and to do so from the framework of your personal values. Reflect and decide for yourself what's worth it and what's not. But it's hard to even realize we need to do these things, and that's the problem. A big part of the work, which most people miss, is going through this thought exercise and having the clarity and self-awareness to see when our efforts are aligned with our personal values and when they're not.

The following three steps can help you to better evaluate and navigate delayed gratification and the associated trade-offs, starting with an assessment of what you're hoping to achieve and why.

1 – Define Your Vision and Know Your Why

Everyone has hopes and dreams, though they can take many different forms. Aspirations may be ambitious or modest, personal or financial, top of mind or suppressed, long-term or short-term, and everything in between. What do they all have in common? Achieving anything of significance requires effort and sacrifice on a level commensurate with the magnitude of your ambitions. From the standpoint of delayed gratification, it's important to define your vision as clearly as possible and then dig into how meaningful it is before you start paying the requisite dues. Know exactly what you're chasing, and make sure it's something worthy. On the surface, this may seem like an obvious and simple exercise. But few people are this deliberate, and seeing the true value of any pursuit is challenging.

When I started my real estate company, my primary goal was to be a good provider for my family. To ensure financial stability for myself and my loved ones and relieve the anxieties I'd always had about money. But as my business and the associated challenges grew, it became clear that the monetary ambitions that fueled me early on were too superficial to be a source of true and lasting fulfillment. So even though being a good provider remained important, I found new purpose and inspiration in aspects of my work that touched others, such as transforming distressed properties, improving the communities in which I operated, and creating good jobs, all of which helped sustain my determination and make the journey more rewarding. Eventually I stepped back from day-to-day operations, empowered the people around me, and focused more on providing strategic direction and advice. I found deeper meaning in a life of contribution—writing books, mentoring, partnering, and otherwise supporting younger and less experienced people embarking on their own journeys. And as often tends to be the case, shifting my attention to helping others yielded even greater abundance.

> "All good things have come to me since
> I no longer seek them for myself."
> —*Saint John of the Cross*

What I learned is that materialistic goals alone are rarely enough to provide long-term motivation and satisfaction. Nor are they likely to be worth the trade-offs involved. You are better off aspiring for something with deeper meaning. Whether your goal is grand or modest doesn't matter. It's more important to know your "why" and find purpose in the process because life is more about the journey than the destination. The process is more important than the outcome. Focus on perfecting your craft rather than on the end result. Fall in love with the work. Lean into the growth. Success and happiness are born of the daily struggles and small victories as you ascend the mountain. And it's those steady steps of progress toward a meaningful objective that fuel you. They also harden your resolve. All of which sustains you over the long haul and provides fulfillment.

> "If you can wake up every morning smiling and
> excited about the day, you're a success."
> —*Mark Cuban*

Almost every goal I've achieved has felt fleeting and hollow relative to everything that went into getting there. Rarely does a lofty milestone live up to expectations. In the words of writer and philosopher Robert M. Pirsig, "The only Zen you can find on the tops of mountains is the Zen you bring up there." In fact, achieving a big goal can actually create a void and leave you feeling down. Most of us spend too much time fixated on the horizon instead of savoring the inherent beauty of what we're experiencing at any given point in time. Author Annie Dillard wrote that "how we spend our days is, of course, how we spend our lives." Setting your sights on a meaningful goal that provides fulfillment along the way is one of the most important keys to harnessing delayed gratification in a healthy and effective way. Another is to avoid sacrificing the things that are most precious.

2 – Sacrifice Intentionally

If you're devoting additional resources to something, whether it be your money, time, or both, what are the implications? What are you forgoing? What activities will be replaced by your efforts? And how will it affect your health and well-being? Your relationships? There are only so many hours in the day, so everything you do comes at a cost. Literally one minute spent on something new displaces something old. So what are you prepared to give up in pursuit of your dreams?

Sacrifices should be made with intention instead of just letting things fall by the wayside of their own accord. Why? Because otherwise it's too easy to get it wrong. Though it may seem obvious, the best things to give up are those we might be better off without. For example, a few of the activities I dramatically reduced (or eliminated) in pursuit of my real estate goals include news consumption, video games, social media, and alcohol. Not only did these changes free up time and money for my business, but they improved my overall well-being. As mentioned, I also curtailed unnecessary spending. I lived modestly and still drove a pickup truck at a stage when other investors were buying flashy sports cars. But limiting indulgences and having less "stuff" doesn't preclude you from leading a joyful life. Nobel Prize winner Pearl S. Buck said that "many people lose the small joys in the hope for the big happiness." But it doesn't have to be that way. For example, my memories of time spent living in a modest rental are just as fond as later memories in a larger home. And I treasure our early family vacations, driving six hours to Cape Cod and staying in a motel, just as dearly as later excursions to Europe, Costa Rica, or Morocco. The everyday activities I most enjoyed didn't cost a lot either. I valued the opportunity to attend your childhood practices, lessons, games, and events. Family movie night at home was just as fun as a trip to the theater. And I loved doing simple things with the family like taking walks, exploring in the woods, going on local beach outings, or even trying to catch frogs and lightning bugs. It may be cliché, but the best things in life really are free.

> "As we get past our superficial material wants and instant gratification, we connect to a deeper part of ourselves, as well as to others, and the universe."
> —*Judith Wright*

What kinds of things should you avoid sacrificing? Anything that undermines your physical or mental health. Your relationships with loved ones. Your faith. Your sense of self, or your values. Basically, anything that will compromise the meaningfulness or length of your life. Remember what is truly precious to you. What costs would be most dire. These priorities should be deeply anchored and fiercely protected. That said, we are all bound by practical constraints, the most notable being how much time is in a day. There will always be trade-offs, like in the chapter's opening story when I was missing the family's morning routine. I certainly didn't take this decision lightly, but responsibly and intentionally striking a balance necessitates some level of sacrifice, even in areas of great import, whether you're working toward a goal or not. And that's okay. But don't use this fact to rationalize unwise decisions or to slide down a slippery slope. Ambitions that will necessitate excessive compromises in your overall well-being should always be approached with the utmost care. And you should look for creative alternatives before making a painful sacrifice.

3 – Creatively Mitigate Trade-Offs

While it may not seem intuitive, creativity and innovation can play a large role in mitigating some of the potential downsides of hard work and delayed gratification. So many of us are wired to look at things as black or white and avoid the grays, and I am no exception. But over time, I have trained myself to think outside the box and always look for creative solutions. Not just because it feels good to solve a problem, but because sometimes you can find ways to "have your cake and eat it too." At least to some extent.

When I started growing my business, I found myself highly motivated to make a better life for myself and my family but unwilling to make some of the compromises that had previously seemed inevitable. Fortunately, as the adage goes, "necessity is the mother of invention." I got resourceful and improvised. For example, in the past I had always kept a wall up between work and home. But I changed that, breaking down those barriers in healthy ways. I embraced my spouse's interest in the business so it became something that we shared instead of something that came between us. I frequently worked from home, and would freely discuss business amongst the family, using it as a tool to help educate, instill values, and inspire. I would also work in the early mornings or late at night, when it was less intrusive. Rather than allowing my work to prevent me from exercising, as I had in the past, I would frequently walk (and sometimes even run) while on the phone, attending to business matters or solving problems. To this day, I have a tendency to pace all over the place whenever I'm on a phone call, stepping outside if I'm in a confined space. While combining these activities still involved a trade-off (my exercise was less meditative), adopting this practice got my body moving and helped me better process things, which fostered creativity and improved decision-making. Almost all of my best and most innovative ideas have come during my walks and runs.

It's a mistake to look at things in a linear way, whether it's delayed gratification or anything in life, for that matter. As we touched on in Chapter 2, there are answers to be found outside of conventional thinking, and they can sometimes help a lot. That doesn't mean sacrifices can be avoided, but they can often be lessened or contained. Work can become obsessive and has a sneaky way of creeping, so I also found it helpful to put up guardrails within which to operate, whether it be doing work at times that by default don't directly interfere with what's most important, or having rules about turning off my phone during certain times. Protecting the sanctity of my greatest priorities not only keeps me grounded but ultimately makes me better at my work.

Doing things like working early and late and curtailing indulgences can seem disagreeable. Such things require patience, fortitude, and discipline. This is one reason why so many people find it more exciting and appealing to adopt a "live for the day" attitude and focus on fostering the more pleasurable aspects of life. While there is merit in this ideal, I believe there is a balance to be struck, and the two approaches don't have to be mutually exclusive. Many sacrifices can be mitigated (and perhaps even beneficial), while the fulfillment of working toward a worthy goal is part of living life to the fullest, especially if you love what you do. Meanwhile, the cost of not pursuing your dreams is as real as any other sacrifice. There is a feeling of loss and emptiness that comes from giving up on something purposeful. From the journey never taken. From a future devoid of what may have come to fruition, whether it be a business, a work of art, financial freedom, or potentially even the opportunity to change the lives of others and make a larger impact on the world around you.

> "Instant gratification is so overrated. It's about the process.
> It's the difficulty. It's the grind of all of it that you better enjoy.
> That's what makes it great."
> —*Bob Myers*

Finally, I would be remiss not to mention two things. First, don't read too much into the personal examples I share in this chapter—the principle of delayed gratification can apply to goals of any shape or size. For example, planting a vegetable garden or learning to play an instrument may provide more personal fulfillment than launching a company or making a lot of money. And that's okay. A goal should always align with the values and wishes of the setter, and the grandiosity of a goal doesn't equate to its worthiness. Second, while evaluating the trade-offs of delayed gratification is unquestionably worthwhile, it's not like doing a math problem. Life is a lot murkier, and it's not easy to weigh things like relationships, life experiences, and personal values. Delayed gratification is nuanced and filled with paradoxes, which can make it tricky to navigate. That's why I experienced so much torment while clearing snow. An anguish that compelled me to shout my frustration into the muffled blackness of a cold and stormy morning. Yes, I had awareness. I knew why I was doing what I was doing. And I realized what sacrifices I was making. I made them deliberately, but I was still plagued with doubts. In the end, this cognizance allowed me to make better choices and navigate a healthier path forward. I went in eyes wide open and made the best decisions possible with the knowledge and experience I had accumulated at that point in my life. And that's all any of us can ever expect of ourselves.

WHAT DO I WANT FOR YOU?

I want you to recognize the astonishing potential power of delayed gratification and, when you deem it appropriate, harness it to achieve your goals.

I want you to choose your goals wisely. To strive for things that are meaningful to you personally and provide intrinsic rewards, while recognizing that the true fulfillment comes from the journey and not the destination.

DELAYED GRATIFICATION

I want you to make deliberate decisions about the sacrifices you make. To be fully aware of what you're giving up and why, and not lose aspects of your life by default. To sacrifice things that don't serve you and seek creative ways to mitigate the cost of things you forgo. To be cautious about undermining the areas of your life that bring meaning, balance, and fulfillment, and to be vigilant in protecting your boundaries.

I want you to decide how to wield delayed gratification by measuring the worth of things on your own personal scale. To weigh sacrifices against potential future outcomes and make the best decisions that you can. And I want you to reap the rewards.

6

DISCOMFORT

Overcoming Fear and Doing Hard Things

> Discomfort is the price of admission to a meaningful life.
> —*Susan David*

> Give vulnerability a shot. Give discomfort its due. Because I think he or she who is willing to be the most uncomfortable is not only the bravest, but rises the fastest.
> —*Tim Ferriss*

I was browsing social media when a video grabbed my attention. A fit, thirty-something man in a purple tee was speaking enthusiastically from up in a tree. And then, in a flash, he was popping out of a car trunk, continuing to talk without pause. And then, in another blink of an eye, the same man was peering out through the opening of a green trash receptacle, wrapping up his message with an infectious smile. Here is what he said:

> What's up, weirdos! This is Mike Posner. And this October my coach Dr. Jon Kedrowski and I are going to be guiding a private trek in Nepal, in the Himalayas, to Everest Base Camp. It's going to be

life-changing. And now you have the opportunity to sign up to trek with us to Everest Base Camp. In Nepal. In the Himalayas. Doing breathwork. Seeing exclusive acoustic concerts from me, Mike Posner. This sh*t's going to be life changing. Go to the link in my bio to apply now.

"Wow," I thought. "What an incredible opportunity." I felt a stirring of interest and excitement. Trekking to Everest Base Camp had been on my bucket list for as long as I could remember, but it had always seemed so distant and out of reach. The video was a bit goofy and playful, but I felt a strong compulsion to learn more. Maybe it was because this was the specific trek I'd always dreamed of, and it seemed like the universe had magically placed it in my path. Maybe it was the idea of visiting a Buddhist country and doing breath work. Maybe it was my recollection of how impressed I had been listening to Mike Posner on the *Rich Roll Podcast*. Maybe it was the fact that the opportunity was being extended to weirdos, which made it seem like a personal invitation to me. Or maybe it was all these things combined. Whatever it was, I felt a strong pull. I quickly navigated my way to the trip website, where I learned that the application process was going to be competitive, and only fifteen people would be chosen. The group would convene in Kathmandu and then take helicopters to the village of Lukla, where the two-week round-trip journey to Everest Base Camp would begin. Over the next few hours, I determinedly worked on my application, answering the essay questions to the best of my ability. When it was complete, I hit submit, and then I waited. A few weeks later I was invited to the second stage in the application process, which was a video interview, and then a couple weeks after that I was selected to go. I couldn't believe it! In just a few months, I'd be headed to Nepal for the adventure of a lifetime.

To say I was excited would be an understatement, but I was also nervous, and my anxieties increased as my departure date approached. Not only was there the physical challenge to consider, but I'd be spending 24-7 with a group of people I'd never met before. I'm also scared of heights, so the idea of hiking along cliffs and crossing suspension bridges was terrifying, not to mention the helicopter rides to and from Lukla, which I had since learned was the most dangerous airport in the world. Finally, if all that weren't enough, I'd be doing the entire trip at high altitude, which comes with a host of risks all its own. All this stuff and more got in my head. Despite my strong desire to go, my fears made me so uncomfortable that I seriously entertained pulling out and not going at all. Fortunately, in the end, I objectively weighed the risks and knew that I couldn't let my fears dictate my decision. I hold a firm belief that it's important to lean into things that make you uncomfortable, because this is where the greatest opportunities for growth are found. This premise had proven true for me time and time again, and I knew that if I backed out of this trip to Nepal, I'd regret it for the rest of my life. So I swallowed my fears and just bucked up and did it.

Turns out that some of my fear was justified, and not everyone who started on that trip would make it to the end.

I reached out and gently grasped my friend Elliot's hand, leaned over his hospital bed, gave him a kiss on the forehead, and spoke softly in his ear. "It's Brian, Elliot. I'm here with you. I want you to know that everything's going to be okay. You're going to be okay."

Despite these words, I was scared because I had serious doubts whether everything would be okay. Yes, I had been nervous about my trek to Everest Base Camp, but it was proving to be far more trying than any of us had imagined. After our hike that day Elliot had fallen gravely ill, eventually losing all coherence. He had developed high altitude cerebral edema (HACE)—a severe and potentially fatal condition brought on by physical exertion at high elevation. Now Elliot was on oxygen at a small village clinic, awaiting medevac to a hospital in Kathmandu. My friend Angel and I had decided to go to the clinic to wish him well and provide comfort, but Elliot was moaning, mumbling, and thrashing around, seemingly unaware of our presence, which was disconcerting.

After offering words of comfort, Angel and I pulled up chairs and decided to stay for a while. And that's when a loud, shrill, continuous beep sounded, and I saw that the monitor displaying Elliot's heartbeat had flatlined. Angel and I jumped up in alarm and frantically called for help. A medic rushed in and quickly determined that a sensor had fallen off when Elliot was thrashing around. He reconnected everything, and Elliot's heartbeat reappeared on the screen. Such a simple thing, but I was now completely freaked out. For a moment, I had thought my worst fears had materialized—that Elliot was going to die. And I couldn't handle it. I told Angel that I was not able to maintain my composure and needed to step out, because if Elliot had any awareness of his surroundings, I didn't want to fall apart in front of him and cause additional distress.

Elliot had been my roommate on the trip, and just a few days earlier I had woken to find him distraught. Someone very close to him had died back home. Elliot had wrestled with what to do, and after much contemplation, he had decided to complete the trek in this person's honor. "It's what he would have wanted," Elliot had told me, and I agreed. And now, despite the assurances of our guides, I didn't know if Elliot was even going to make it back home. It all just seemed so unfair, and there was nothing I could do. I felt sad, worried, frustrated, and helpless. Now, overcome with exhaustion and emotion, I left the clinic, walked out into the dark night, found a place to sit down, buried my head in my hands, and wept.

At first light, Elliot was transported by helicopter to the hospital in Kathmandu, and eventually, after overcoming a host of complications, he returned home to British Columbia and made a full recovery. But the high elevation continued to take a toll on the rest of the group. Most of us dealt with symptoms of altitude sickness to one degree or another, and two more people had to be medevaced. The lower oxygen levels at altitude also made the physical challenge of covering over 120 miles of mountainous terrain more difficult. By the time we arrived at Base Camp, oxygen levels were 50 percent lower than at sea level, which made everything harder. As did the spartan living conditions. For most of the trek, we didn't have heat in our rooms, and at some places we didn't even have electricity or running water. We ate a lot of unfamiliar foods, and the schedule was unpredictable. All of which stood in stark contrast to the creature comforts and routines of my daily, spoiled life back home. But even though I was experiencing discomfort at a level I hadn't felt in years, there were positive sides to the journey. In many ways, it felt like an awakening. Confronted with the harsh realization of how soft I had become, I resolved to embrace and appreciate the challenges I was experiencing.

While such physical hardships tested me, the aspect of the trip that pushed me furthest outside of my comfort zone was the more personal, human side. Being around people 24-7 for two weeks, sharing tight, primitive living quarters, and facing adversities together was challenging. But it also proved worthwhile because the circumstances bonded us and put meaningful connection at the center of the entire experience. Being a strong introvert, I found some of the interpersonal aspects uncomfortable initially, but I embraced this opportunity to engage with my fellow travelers. Friendly banter blossomed into more meaningful conversations about personal life experiences and thought-provoking philosophical debates. I tend to be a private person, so opening up in this way is something I rarely do, but going outside my comfort zone was immensely rewarding. Relating on a deeper level gave me insight into how truly special these people were—it was like uncovering a priceless treasure that had been hidden right in front of me.

My trek to Everest Base Camp was not what I had expected it to be. I had looked forward with great anticipation to experiencing Nepal and seeing the Himalayas. And these things were amazing. But the entire adventure turned out to be so much more. In large part the reason the trip was so impactful is that I was taken further outside my comfort zone, physically, mentally, and emotionally, than I ever could have imagined. But it's precisely because of how big the challenges were that I experienced so much growth and reaped outsized rewards.

The adversities made everything more meaningful and heightened the sense of fulfillment. The sights, sounds and experiences were crisper and more special. The mountains and culture were more raw, stunning, and real. The friendships created were deep enough to last a lifetime. And it all combined to make me feel fully alive, which is a priceless gift in a world where we too often allow ourselves to fall into unhealthy but comfortable ruts. The trip was a life-changing experience that I will benefit from moving forward, perhaps in ways that I still can't fathom. And none of it would have been possible if I had been unwilling to do uncomfortable things.

While my trip to Nepal may be one of the more profound examples, I can say that every meaningful achievement and growth experience in my life has required me to go well outside of my comfort zone. The challenges that each of us face generate fear, and overcoming them requires us to endure things that are uncomfortable. But I've learned that making the effort, while not easy, is almost always worth it. There are great rewards on the other side of our anxieties, and the benefits are usually commensurate with the level of discomfort endured. It's like when you climb a mountain—the higher you go, the more difficult it is, but the views are better. Life is the same way. The more uncomfortable you get, the deeper you have to dig, the more you endure, the greater the growth.

> "If you want to live life, go out there, get cold, get hungry, get scratched up, take those sunrises in, see the sunsets as blessings, and push yourself a little bit beyond what you think you can do."
> —*Conrad Anker*

Unfortunately, the correlation between discomfort and growth was not clear to me until later in life. In fact, when I was a twenty-one-year-old freshly minted college grad overflowing with ambition, my view of discomfort was almost exactly the opposite of what it is today—I thought of discomfort as something to be avoided at all costs. To be fair, I had just finished putting myself through school by working multiple jobs, some of which felt miserable at the time. Among other things, I washed dishes in a dining hall, loaded trucks for UPS, served hot dogs at a concession stand, and made cold calls trying to sell lawncare services. Despite my best efforts, I had a difficult time making ends meet. My mattress rested directly on the floor because I couldn't afford a box spring or a bed frame, and I used old milk crates for my nightstand and dresser. And when the Burger King near campus had a two-burgers-for-a-buck special, I spent twenty dollars for forty hamburgers. I ate one and froze the rest, then microwaved them one at a time for meals over the following weeks, a strategy that I thought was ingenious, but my roommates found appalling.

Coming from this backdrop, my dream was to make as much money as possible in order to live a soft and comfortable life. And if the gods smiled upon me, maybe even one of luxury and leisure. This seemed like a sensible aspiration, but in hindsight I can say that such a notion was naive. Yes, I faced adversities in college, but what I didn't appreciate at the time was how much growth I was experiencing as a result. Among other things, I gained valuable skills, developed a strong work ethic, and got a large enough dose of humility to last a lifetime. And while I spent much of my college years dreaming of a better life, I'd eventually reminisce about those same days with fondness and gratitude for the aliveness and the growth. I was experiencing life in its fullest sense, including the difficulties and the rewards, the highs and the lows that bring everything into sharper relief.

> "The most fascinating lesson I've learned about life
> is that the struggle is good."
> —*Joe Rogan*

Most of the growth I experienced after college was also the result of doing hard things—both personally and professionally. Advancing in the business world required me to go well outside of my comfort zone, particularly when it came to networking and public speaking, which had always terrified me. In high school I was voted "shyest" in my graduating class, and there was nothing that scared me more than getting up in front of a crowd, a fear that continued throughout college and the first decade of my career. I can still remember the first time I had to give a presentation to the executive leadership team of the technology company where I worked. We were at an off-site management retreat in Miami, and I was sitting outside by the hotel swimming pool, panic-stricken, profusely sweating, trying frantically to pull myself together before the presentation started. I was so visibly distressed that a concerned colleague bought me a large margarita and insisted I drink it in a misguided attempt to settle my nerves (not an effective strategy, by the way). But after a few years of practice, my public speaking improved, and I began to speak at conferences, eventually emerging as the company's de facto media spokesperson. Despite my growth it was still uncomfortable, and when I was getting ready to be interviewed on CNN, my nerves made me so nauseous that I had to run into the bathroom right before going on the air. Facing such situations tested me, but each time I did so, I was exercising a muscle that got stronger. Over the ensuing years, I progressively did more interviews and speaking engagements, and then I started teaching, which put me in front of classrooms and auditoriums on a regular basis. Each time I faced my discomfort, it got a little easier, and I can now get up in front of thousands of people and speak without fear, something I never would have dreamed possible in my youth.

> "As you move outside of your comfort zone, what was once the unknown and frightening becomes your new normal."
> —*Robin Sharma*

Starting my own business is another example of something that required me to go outside my comfort zone. I bought my first investment property against the advice of more experienced people, who told me I was making a mistake. Moving forward required me to muster up the courage to overcome a mind plagued with doubts and fear. I was risking my entire life savings, but I was also highly determined. I elected to trust my intuition, which told me to think big and take the risk, even though it might be scary or defy convention. While I faced many challenges, ultimately it was a decision that led to a lot of growth, both personally and professionally. That said, stretching in this manner is not for everyone, and there is absolutely nothing wrong with staying within your vocational comfort zone. But such a choice should be made deliberately and for the right reasons, such as genuine fulfillment and contentment with the status quo—not out of fear or doubts about your capacity to do something difficult.

> "Don't confuse comfort with happiness."
> —*Dean Karnazes*

While the examples I've shared are more career oriented, the same principles apply to other areas of life. For instance, I would discover that enduring the discomfort of physical exercise such as running would produce a host of health benefits and improve my quality of life. And when I stepped out of my comfort zone and allowed myself to be vulnerable in social situations, the rewards were even more plentiful. It's uncomfortable for me to open up and extend myself to others, but it's also the only way to connect and develop meaningful relationships. I remember seeing my future wife for the first time at a running club. I was so intimidated and afraid to speak with her, but I also knew that if I didn't try, I'd be filled with regrets. In this case and many others, if I had stayed in my comfort zone, I would never have met the people who've had the most positive and enduring influence on my life. I would never have experienced love or fatherhood.

On an emotional level, doing uncomfortable things will often create a feeling of accomplishment and fulfillment, which in turn boosts self-esteem. Experiencing hardship also fosters a sense of gratitude for the blessings in life and enables us to feel the good things in a more visceral way than someone trapped in a softer, bubble-wrapped existence. Ensconced in comforts, it's too easy to lose perspective and take things for granted. And if you smooth all the bumps, ridges, and sharp edges out of life, it has no depth or character. There is less contrast, and the brilliance of life is muted and dulled.

While the benefits of going outside your comfort zone are plentiful, that doesn't mean that you should live in a perpetual state of discomfort or do things that are hazardous to your mental or physical well-being. Sound judgement should always prevail—be prudent about the timing and nature of the actions you take. As my experience in Nepal demonstrated, sometimes fear is merited, and there are times that we all need the safety and familiarity of our comfort zones. But there is a balance to be struck because growth requires you to stretch and reach for things that test you in different ways.

Is it easy to move outside of our comfort zone? To lean into hard things? Absolutely not, and that's why it's uncommon—very few people have the courage and discipline to tolerate discomfort, let alone seek it out. But if you can do so, it will set you apart. It will unleash your full potential. Does doing uncomfortable things always work out? That depends on how you look at it. I would argue that, while doing something difficult doesn't always yield the desired outcome, benefits can always be realized. If you end up failing, there are lessons to be learned that can then be applied moving forward. And each time you do something that challenges you, it gets easier, affording you the opportunity to experience the rewards more frequently and intensely. In aggregate, the benefits of seeking discomfort are more than worth the effort. Those few who have the discipline and courage to do uncomfortable things are generously rewarded, both materially and in other less tangible but more meaningful ways.

> "Be willing to be uncomfortable. Be comfortable being uncomfortable. It may get tough, but it's a small price to pay for living a dream."
> —*Peter McWilliams*

In the end, doing uncomfortable things is an opportunity. An opportunity to expand physical, mental, and emotional boundaries. An opportunity to live a fuller and more fulfilling life. And this is where I find myself today. I've come full circle from those college days. I have more experience and a higher level of consciousness. I am disillusioned with an overly comfortable life, and I've built up my ability to selectively embrace things that challenge me. To actively seek discomfort—whether it's a cold plunge, an ultramarathon, meeting new people, manual labor, or a trek to Mount Everest. I do it with purpose and intention. Because I know what the rewards are, and I also know what life is like without testing your boundaries.

WHAT DO I WANT FOR YOU?

I want you to recognize that we live in a world where the natural tendency is to ensconce ourselves in comfort, but for you to know better and have the will to resist.

I want you to face and overcome your fears. To have the courage to lean into things that are safe but uncomfortable physically, mentally, and emotionally. To put yourself in trying circumstances and do hard things.

I want you to build up your tolerance for discomfort by trying things you're afraid of or that seem disagreeable. Strike up a conversation with a stranger. Take a cold shower. Go on a camping trip. Take chances. Test yourself. Expand your boundaries.

I want you to experience the amazing and indelible effects of doing uncomfortable things. The growth. The fulfillment and confidence. The abundance and vitality that can only come from living all aspects of life, including those parts that challenge you.

7

YOU ARE ENOUGH

The Challenge of Knowing, Being, and Loving Yourself

> It is not the end of the physical body that should worry us.
> Rather, our concern must be to live while we're alive—to release
> our inner selves from the spiritual death that comes with
> living behind a facade designed to conform to external definitions
> of who and what we are.
> —*Elisabeth Kübler-Ross*

> Let it go, let it go, you are enough
> So we let our shadows fall away like dust.
> —*Ryan Curtis O'Neal*

I scanned the room and made eye contact with each of my friends. We were sitting in a circle on the floor in the penthouse of the Aloft Hotel in Kathmandu. Having just finished a magical trek to Mount Everest Base Camp, we were reflecting on the journey and sharing our takeaways from the experience. Our time together in Nepal was coming to a close, and Mike Posner, who (together with Dr. Jon Kedrowski) had orchestrated this entire experience, had just led us through a Wim Hof breathing exercise. The breath work and this sharing circle were designed to be our "off-ramp" and help us with the transition back to our everyday lives.

I listened as my companions, one by one, shared their thoughts and gratitude. I was moved by their sentiments and vulnerability—it was clear that the trip had deeply affected everyone, and I was no exception. It was now my turn to speak, and I was nervous. But as I looked around the room, the warmth and kindness were palpable. These people had been strangers just two weeks ago, but living together, facing adversity, experiencing the wonders of Nepal, and the long, deep conversations over dozens of meals and arduous, dusty trails had forged a bond that was surprisingly strong. They may have started the trek as strangers, but they now felt like family.

So, with a voice trembling with emotion, I shared what was in my heart. "I've dreamed of doing the trek to Everest Base Camp for a very long time—it was on my bucket list," I said. "And the reasons seemed obvious. I wanted to witness the incredible natural beauty of the Himalayas. I wanted to visit the villages along the way and experience the culture. But a few days before I left on this trip, a friend reached out to wish me well, and he shared some words of wisdom. He told me to remember that it's often more about the *who* than the *what*. And then he said, 'There is someone on this trip who needs to meet you. And someone you need to meet.'"

I hesitated for a moment, and then continued. "The trek was everything I had always dreamed it would be. It was so beautiful. But it turned out that my friend was right . . ." I paused again, summoning the courage to look them all in the eyes. "By far the best part of this entire trip was you guys. And I didn't see that coming."

I explained that while I have achieved a lot professionally over the years, and I'm grateful for that, at times it's put me in aggressive environments and situations that were not well aligned with who I am as a person, which made it more difficult to open up and trust people. It exacerbated a tendency toward hypervigilance, making it harder to let go and just be myself.

"Hearing my friend's advice before I arrived here," I said, "I decided that I would make it a priority to extend myself to the people around me on this trip. That I would do the best I could to open up and just be me. And you guys made that easy. From our first day when we did a breath-work session together that brought up so much emotion, you all contributed to an environment that felt safe. I'm so grateful for that."

I looked around the room and saw that my words had touched my friends. I proceeded to explain that while I'm proud of what I've accomplished in my career, I didn't always do things for the right reasons. "Sometimes I think I feared that I wasn't enough," I confided. "That if I didn't do great things, and be the best, that people wouldn't respect me or like me. But when I met you guys, you accepted me for who I am, without knowing anything about my professional achievements," I said.

Now I paused for a few seconds, reflecting briefly on something that had transpired early in the trip. Something that Mike Posner had reminded me of and shared with us when he had addressed the group just moments before. Mike is an accomplished musical artist—a multiplatinum singer and songwriter. But on one of the first days of our trek I had confided with him that I really hadn't had any familiarity with his music prior to the trip. I knew of him from listening to a podcast in which he had discussed his walk across America and his plans to summit Mount Everest. I recalled that he had demonstrated a humility, vulnerability, and strength that I admired. He just seemed like a beautiful soul. A good human being. I had decided he was someone worth following because of *who* he was as a person, not because of his accomplishments as a musician, and that's how I ended up here. A few days later, Mike learned more about my own professional achievements, and afterward, he had made a point to pull me aside and share with me that he felt the same way. He had grown to like me without any knowledge of the books I had published or my success in the real estate world. His words and the kindness of his gesture had moved me more than I think he realized. He was telling me that I am enough.

I looked to my right and made direct eye contact with Mike, who was sitting next to me. "And that's why what you said to me earlier in the trip was so meaningful to me," I said. I paused for a moment before returning my attention to the rest of the group. "Spending the past couple of weeks with you all, I've been able to be myself . . . and it felt so good," I said. Overcome with emotion, I thanked them. I could feel the tears running freely down my cheeks, and my heart was full. Mike leaned over and gave me a hug. I couldn't have asked for a more perfect off-ramp.

Moments like the one I experienced in that sharing circle in Kathmandu are special to me, for many reasons. Perhaps the biggest is that there are few gifts in this world as precious as feeling seen, accepted, and even loved for who you genuinely are. Having the courage to open yourself up, put yourself out there, and experience true connection with others can be a deeply fulfilling experience. But unfortunately, such occurrences are all too rare for most of us because, at some point, we have lost our way. Our fears and egos have dug a neat little hole, thrown our true selves in there, and buried them, one shovelful of dirt at a time, which not only obfuscates our relationships, but slowly smothers our souls.

Too many people invest an inordinate amount of time and energy crafting lives designed to climb ladders or gain the approval of others. And I am no exception. At various points in my career, I allowed myself to get immersed in environments that were out of alignment with my values, and I would sometimes respond by contorting myself in a manner that, in my skewed assessment, would allow me to thrive. I tried to be perfect. To prove myself and be more, because I didn't think I was enough. At no point in my life was such destructive behavior more evident than during my early thirties, when I took a job in the tech sector. Working there was like being slowly baked in a kiln. It hardened me. But it also put cracks in me. Cracks through which the toxicity of the workplace seeped in and manifested itself in a host of ugly ways. There were many casualties and consequences of this experience, including the drastic deterioration of my health (see Chapter 9), but perhaps the worst outcome was that I lost a part of my *self*. I found myself changing. Adapting. And it was an ugly mutation. I was more aggressive, more Machiavellian, and more self-centered. I was less kind, less patient, and less compassionate. The first time I had to lay someone off at that company, I was sympathetic and, after delivering the news, I broke down. I felt so bad about it that I couldn't sleep for days. Faced with the same situation just a couple of years later, I had become calloused and numb. My message was curt and matter-of-fact. I displayed little-to-no emotion, promptly returned to my work, and pushed the layoff out of my mind.

It feels oppressive to live a life that's not in alignment with your authentic self. Existing in a state of incongruence is like wearing a thick, heavy suit of armor that covers you from head to toe. It's stifling. It chafes and makes you sweat too much. It's draining. And it's not worth it. Any external validation you might receive in response to a façade is hollow because, deep down, you know it's based on an illusion. The positive feelings that such responses may or may not generate are a dopamine hit that fades as quickly as the burst of flame from a struck match. Then you are left with nothing more than a fleeting swirl of smoke. Followed by emptiness.

> "To be yourself in a world that is constantly trying to make you something else is the greatest accomplishment."
> —*Ralph Waldo Emerson*

Why do so many of us conduct ourselves in such a shallow, self-destructive fashion? To start with, there is a cacophony of forces outside of ourselves pressuring us to be something we're not. It might be the expectations of others, societal norms, our workplace culture, the marketing messages we're incessantly barraged with, or, more likely, a combination of these and other factors. We're instilled with misplaced beliefs that superficial things like professional achievements, money, or popularity will make us happier. That they will bring the peace and fulfillment that can only come from within. Such notions can be as compelling and alluring as they are misguided, and compromising ourselves can seem a worthy price. Meanwhile, our will to resist such influences and stay true to ourselves is subverted by fear. Fear that I've experienced many times. Fear that we all share. Fear of not being enough. Fear of the hurt caused by judgment, ostracism, rejection, or abandonment. So what do we do? We conform with outside influences and encapsulate ourselves in that heavy suit of armor. An armor designed to protect ourselves as we pursue our ego-driven quests. But in doing so we are unwittingly suffocating ourselves. We're blocking out the oxygen necessary for us to breathe. The oxygen necessary for our internal flame to burn bright. Eventually, that fire within dims until there is nothing left but a small ember.

> "It is difficult to find happiness within oneself,
> but it is impossible to find it anywhere else."
> —*Arthur Schopenhauer*

Too often, people don't take steps to rekindle that internal flame until the weight of incongruence and duplicity is too heavy to bear any longer. Just like me, they reach a breaking point. When the burden becomes unsustainable, you're forced to either muster up the courage and fortitude to make the necessary changes, or things deteriorate to a point of tragic consequences. While such a fate may seem overly extreme or unlikely, everyone loses their way at times to one extent or another. And when it happens, finding your way back is not easy. But there are three steps you can take to do a better job than I did, and I've outlined them below.

1 – Awareness

The most important key to both finding and sustaining your true self is to have a higher level of consciousness—a greater awareness of what's going on, both inside yourself and in the world around you. To know that there is a war that is being waged. That our true selves are constantly under assault by a myriad of internal and external forces working to change who we are at our core. It's difficult to win any battle if you don't even know you're under attack. Such things may seem obvious, but they weren't always apparent to me. The kiln I was in heated up slowly, and I had a lot of companions on my path to self-destruction. Engaging in behaviors with a group can normalize your conduct and distort your perspective. Ironically, I was able to clearly see the detrimental effects of a toxic workplace on one of my friends, even though I couldn't see it in myself. She had worked with me before, and I helped recruit her to join the tech firm shortly after I did. After a couple of years, I realized how much she had changed, and not in a good way. She worked in sales, where there was ruthless competition and strong incentives to land deals, and it seemed to me like she had lost her moral compass. Like she was selling her soul, along with our company's products. Concerned about her welfare, and missing the old version of her, I shared my concerns. Unsurprisingly, they were not well received. In hindsight, it's pretty clear why. Confronting her about how much she had changed smacked of moral superiority, and was one of the most hypocritical things I've done, given my own sorry state of affairs. I was so blind.

To be fair, the entire concept of "self" was relatively foreign to me at that age, and not something I gave deliberate consideration to. While I certainly wanted to be a good person, my views were far more outwardly focused. At that point in time, I was primarily driven (and sometimes blinded) by extrinsic goals. If I'd had even the most rudimentary level of awareness, not only would I have quit that job sooner, but I would never have taken it in the first place.

> "The secret is to have a sense of yourself, your real self, your unique self. And not just once in a while, or once a day, but all through the day, the week and life."
> —*Bill Murray*

Pretty much every aspect of finding and maintaining our true selves starts with a more awakened existence. Looking deeply inward, while remaining cognizant of what's going on around you. Being mindful. Being vigilant. Being deliberate. Having this level of consciousness is the first step toward any area of personal growth. It's the biggest step. And it's the most powerful step. Because without awareness, there is no step at all. We're ignorantly caught up in the current of forces outside ourselves, unmoored and floating without any direction or purpose. And that current can take us in any direction it wants.

2 – Self-Exploration

After awareness, the next step is self-exploration and deliberately directing energy toward fueling the ember of true self that resides within each of us. Slipping off the armor. Stripping away the layers of life's corruption and allowing some of the early innocence and exuberance of youth to resurface. Exploring who you really are requires a great deal of personal introspection and can be effectively undertaken using the same approaches as your exploration of childhood (Chapter 1). Be open and look deep inside yourself. As Chinese philosopher Lao Tzu said, "At the center of your being you have the answer; you know who you are and you know what you want." Take note of what drains you versus what fills you with positive energy, then move toward the good stuff. Nourish these things—they will allow your true self to emerge and to shine. You'll know what feels right. We tend to naturally gravitate toward those aspects of life and activities that bring us genuine joy, fulfillment, and inner harmony. You just need to be open to receiving the messages. To break free of the inertia pulling you in the wrong direction and listen to your heart. To breathe, trust your intuition, and let yourself go there.

> "Have the courage to follow your heart and intuition. They somehow already know what you truly want to become. Everything else is secondary."
> —*Steve Jobs*

After I quit my toxic job, running played a significant role in getting me back on a better path. I leaned into this activity because it just felt right. Even in the earliest days of my childhood, running filled me with joy. It was an integral part of almost all my favorite activities—outdoor games, sports, and life in general. As a kid, I'd run or ride my bike almost every place I went, and I particularly loved to run, play, and explore in the woods, where I felt safe and most at peace, which probably explains my eventual gravitation toward trail running and ultramarathons. In addition to the physical benefits, returning to this activity settled my mind and grounded me, restoring equanimity. Running is also meditative. Another activity that brings me the joy of childhood is playing board games, which I now own in prodigious quantities. The "play" element of board games is certainly fun, but I find the quality interaction it can provide with loved ones even more fulfilling. Bringing healthy activities such as these back into my life and taking time to reflect was healing and brought me into better alignment. It also helped me gain clarity with regards to what kinds of work I wanted to do moving forward. I would soon start to teach, which I found fulfilling, and I eventually started several of my own businesses, which also felt right because it gave me more control over my own destiny and afforded me the opportunity to create healthier work environments and make a positive difference in the lives of others. I was able to operate in a manner that was consistent with my core values.

3 – Acceptance and Love

Once you achieve a higher level of awareness and self-knowledge, the more challenging but necessary next step is acceptance. Exercising self-compassion and learning to love yourself is something I've struggled with my whole life. And I am not alone. Why is it so damn hard? It may be an oversimplification, but many of us just don't believe we're enough. Whether it's a result of our life experiences, things we've been told by others, or the voices in our heads, we hold ourselves to unreasonably high standards. And if we're not enough for ourselves, how can we believe we're enough for others? That we're worthy of love?

Though it may sound overly contrite or simplistic, we're all worthy of love. Strip away all the window dressing, remove the insecurities and self-protection mechanisms developed in response to the craziness of this world and the hardships we've experienced, and, at our core, we are all enough. *You* are enough. We each have our own uniqueness, passions, gifts, imperfections, values, and things that bring us energy and fulfillment. Even if it's buried deeper in some than others, there is also an innocence, goodness, and beauty within each of us. A light that can be uncovered, dusted off, and shine bright again. Identifying that about yourself and truly believing it will allow you to be free. Free to lead a life in better alignment with your true self. Free to be happier. To be more at peace.

> "You yourself, as much as anybody in the entire universe, deserve your love and affection."
> —*Buddha*

Is it easy to live a life of true authenticity? To know you are enough and love yourself? Not at all. It's a journey that I'm still on. Will you encounter resistance? Absolutely. Will everyone accept you for who you are? No, unfortunately, but I want you to know that's okay.

Knowing you are enough and loving yourself is a deep source of energy that can give you the strength to keep your flame burning bright. It will open the door to meeting kindred spirits and people attracted to the light you bring to the world. You'll encounter fellow humans who fuel your fire and fill your soul. And you'll experience connections that are more beautiful than even the Himalayas.

WHAT DO I WANT FOR YOU?

I want you to recognize and resist the strong influences working to change you and lead you astray. To take the time to really know yourself and follow your inner compass. Lean into those things that bring you joy, peace, and fulfillment.

I want you to find the strength of will to walk the path of life on your own terms. To live a life that is as closely in alignment with your genuine self as possible. I want you to know that one of the greatest gifts that you can give yourself is to just be you.

I want you to recognize that happiness can only come from within. To strive for self-acceptance and show yourself the same compassion you hold for others. To love yourself. To know with deep conviction that *you are enough*.

8

GRATITUDE

A Priceless Treasure Free for the Taking

> Whatever we are waiting for—peace of mind, contentment, grace, the inner awareness of simple abundance—it will surely come to us, but only when we are ready to receive it with an open and grateful heart.
> —*Sarah Ban Breathnach*

> I cried because I had no shoes, then I met a man who had no feet.
> —*Helen Keller*

When the starting gun went off and I began running, I felt a sense of resolve and calm that was unlike anything I had experienced in prior races. I had a singular purpose centered around John Einbeck—my company's first employee and a trusted friend who was battling cancer. John had taken a turn for the worse—the cancer had spread into his spine, and he could no longer walk. John was such a strong and energetic person that this reality was difficult for those of us who knew him to wrap our heads around.

Running a race while still trying to process John's debilitation made me feel a sense of privilege and gratitude beyond measure. I knew John was deeply suffering and would give anything to be able to walk again, let alone run. Yet here I was running a race. It was a priceless gift. I resolved to honor John by thinking of him throughout the race and deeply embracing the sincerest gratitude for being alive and healthy. Not only was I able to walk, but I could run. I was humbled by the magnitude of such a blessing.

During the race, I maintained my focus on gratitude with each step I took. Any aches and pains that surfaced were welcomed as a gift that I knew John would give anything to feel. It was a hilly course, but on that day, I felt a lightness and ease in my running that I had never experienced before. Despite the fact that I was in my midforties and well beyond my prime, it would be the fastest half marathon I ever ran in my life, by a significant margin.

When John passed, I delivered a eulogy at his funeral and dedicated a book to him. He may have lost his battle with cancer, but he lives on in my heart as a reminder to stay grateful.

In the years following John's passing, I continued running and racing. After nearly a decade of training, running had become a core element of my well-being, providing balance in my life and offering a host of physical and mental benefits. I also found it rewarding to challenge myself, competing in marathons and trying to improve my speed. So when I pulled up short on a long run with an excruciating pain in my back, I was concerned. And when the pain persisted for days and then weeks afterward, I was downright alarmed.

What followed were multiple doctors visits, extensive tests, and prolonged bouts of severe pain. I was diagnosed with degenerative disk disease and told that the only options available to me revolved around pain management. For a full year, I slept on the floor, flat on my back—the only position that would afford me enough relief to get any rest. No longer able to run, I began taking long walks, and that sustained me.

After a year of suffering, I found myself at a medical appointment unrelated to my back, and ended up discussing my running history and back issues with the doctor, who was also a runner and empathized with my situation. He had dealt with a similar issue and told me about a highly regarded running clinic, encouraging me to make an appointment despite my prior diagnosis.

My visit to the clinic gave me new hope. I was carefully examined by a physical therapist who specialized in the rehabilitation of running injuries, and he expressed confidence that if I followed his guidance, I'd be able to recover and run again. And he was right—over the ensuing months of physical therapy, my pain subsided and I was gradually able to resume running. It seemed like a miracle. And with that miracle came some tangible changes. For one, I stopped wearing a watch. It just seemed pointless to care about how fast or far I ran, when I could just run. It was pure joy. From that point forward I would view races less as a competition and more as an opportunity to celebrate my ability to run. And I soon found myself lured into the woods and running on trails, an environment that brought me great peace. Yes, I had been grateful to run before, but my gratitude now reached new heights and has stayed there. As my endurance improved, I ventured into the mountains and ran for longer and longer distances, enjoying the beauty of the nature while relishing the new physical challenges. And whenever it felt difficult, I repeated a mantra that I've now fully embraced: "I get to do this."

The concept of gratitude is one that I didn't deliberately contemplate for the first four decades of my life. That doesn't mean that I didn't understand the notion or appreciate things. Humble beginnings provided a solid foundation for recognizing the many blessings I experienced and helped me to maintain perspective. And my service as a Peace Corps volunteer further deepened my appreciation for the luxuries and privileges most of us enjoy but sometimes take for granted. But there is a difference between feeling gratitude when prompted by specific encounters or profound experiences and adopting gratitude as a practice. Only by making gratitude part of your daily life can you reap the full benefits. I was too slow to make conscious efforts to understand the power of gratitude and incorporate it into my mentality—to harness it as an effective tool to better my everyday life. This was a mistake, and one it would take time to rectify.

My first foray into the practice of gratitude was through journaling. I chose a daily journal with gratitude prompts, starting and ending each day with a positive affirmation and reflection on things I'm grateful for. I found that practicing gratitude in this manner set the tone for the day ahead, or allowed me to be more at peace going to bed—both of which helped manifest feelings of gratitude throughout the rest of the day. My gratitude journal entries will often include meaningful events, people, or things that I experience: maybe family members or friends, fun times, overcoming a challenge, or some good fortune that came my way. These are perhaps the more obvious things to be grateful for. But I quickly realized that it is equally (if not more) helpful to acknowledge all the little things that can bring joy into our lives. Things that we feel or experience that may on their surface seem less consequential. Like the warm feeling of sunshine, a moment of inner peace, the laughter of a child, or the song of a bird.

> "He is a wise man who does not grieve for the things which he has not, but rejoices for those which he has."
> —*Epictetus*

Gratitude has a tendency to be ephemeral, the thoughts and feelings slipping away as quickly as they arise, so capturing your gratitude in an enduring way can help provide an antidote to this, whether it be through journaling, writing on slips of paper that you collect in a jar, or dictating to your phone. Such practices can make the benefits more lasting and afford the opportunity to later revisit the many things you are grateful for, reflecting and gaining the benefit of them again in the future.

It can also be constructive to engage with others in your gratitude practices. For example, you can make a commitment to expressing your gratitude to at least one person every day. It can be a thank you offered in response to someone's kind gesture, or telling someone, "I appreciate you." And if you're in a relationship, it can be nourishing to engage in a gratitude practice with your partner, in which you commit to sharing gratitude on a regular schedule—whether it's in the form of an appreciation for one another, an expression of gratitude for other things in your life, or both. In the words of writer William Arthur Ward, "Feeling gratitude and not expressing it is like wrapping a present and not giving it."

An expression of appreciation is certainly a gift you can give to others, but the benefits go far deeper. Yes, you can lift up those around you with kind words and gestures of gratitude, and that's a beautiful thing, but the effects on your own wellness can be more profound. Author Amy Collette calls gratitude "the spark that lights a fire of joy in your soul." Gratitude practices have been linked with a wide range of personal benefits, including improved mental health, better relationships, and even physical well-being. *Reader's Digest* newsletter *The Healthy* reported that practicing gratitude has been shown in hundreds of studies to have wide-ranging health benefits such as lowering blood pressure, increasing immune function, improving cognition, boosting mood, improving sleep, reducing chronic pain, and lowering inflammation.[1] The same article reported that an "analysis of dozens of cardiovascular health studies found that people at risk of a heart attack who had some sort of gratitude practice showed improved heart health and a lower risk of heart disease."

Such studies and claims may be difficult to believe, but what they boil down to is the incredible power of the mind and our body's physiological responses to our mental and emotional states, a principle that is well-established and at the heart of Dr. Bessel van der Kolk's bestselling book *The Body Keeps the Score*. Basically, any practice that can foster positivity and peace of mind will eventually manifest itself in healthy ways within your body (the reverse is also true). Based on my personal experience, the far-reaching benefits of gratitude should not be underestimated, including both the physical and mental benefits. Embracing gratitude can change how you think and how you view the world. It is arguably the practice that has brought me the greatest rewards of any single self-improvement initiative I have undertaken.

> "Wear gratitude like a cloak, and it will feed every corner of your life."
> —*Rumi*

WHAT DO I WANT FOR YOU?

I want you to recognize the many tangible benefits of practicing gratitude and see it for what it is—a priceless treasure that is available to you and free for the taking. Don't wait as long as I did to make a conscious effort to understand the power and importance of embracing gratitude in your life. Focus more on what you have than what you lack. Recognize the many blessings that we all enjoy, and adopt a gratitude mindset.

I want you to consider adopting a gratitude practice in some form and incorporating it into your routine. Whether you write down the things you're grateful for, speak them aloud, or recite them internally is less important than that you establish a habit that you can sustain. Regardless of what methods you choose to employ, I want you to make a deliberate effort to start feeling gratitude more often, especially for those little moments that may go unnoticed by others, but will add up over time.

I want you to lean into those feelings of gratitude and allow them to come out in how you react to things, what you choose to do, and how you communicate and interact with those around you. To not leave sentiments unspoken. To give the gift of gratitude to others by thanking people more frequently and telling them that you appreciate them.

Finally, I want you to experience the magical benefits that feeling and expressing sincere gratitude can foster in your life. To feel the peace and joy that it can bring, and to share that light with the world.

9

HEALTH SPAN

Living the Longest, Happiest, and Healthiest Life

> It is health that is real wealth and not pieces of gold and silver.
> —*Mahatma Gandhi*

> Keeping your body healthy is an expression of gratitude to the whole cosmos—the trees, the clouds, everything.
> —*Thích Nhất Hạnh*

The doctor was studying my test results with an intensity and a deep frown that made me uneasy. A few days prior I had been rushed to the emergency room after experiencing intense chest pains and having trouble breathing. After I arrived at the hospital, they ran a full battery of diagnostics and held me for observation before determining that I wasn't in immediate danger and sending me home. Now I was on my follow-up visit, hoping to get a better understanding of what had happened.

At thirty-five years old, it seemed unlikely that I had experienced a heart attack, and they had confirmed as much at the hospital. But something was clearly not right. People don't get severe chest pains for no reason. I knew that my health had badly deteriorated since I had taken a job at a tech start-up five years prior. My work there had been all-consuming. It was a high stress environment that encouraged long work hours with a hard-charging culture, break rooms stocked with every junk food imaginable, kegs of beer on tap, and late-night restaurant food deliveries to the office for everyone who was still grinding away. By the time I found myself in the doctor's office I had gained nearly fifty pounds and was barely recognizable to anyone who'd known me before.

Even though the doctor had already reviewed my results once, he kept flipping back and forth between pages, raising his bushy eyebrows, making facial expressions and noises that reflected his disapproval. None of this did anything to ease my already frayed nerves.

"Listen," said the doctor in a stern voice. "The first thing to know is that you're going to be okay . . ." The surge of relief at hearing these words was muted by the doctor's seriousness, and the relief was short-lived. "At least for now," he added. He furrowed his brow and glanced back down at the test results. "I think the pain you experienced was caused by pericarditis. And that the chest pains may have triggered a panic attack. Have you been under a lot of stress lately?" he asked.

I shared with the doctor that yes, my work was stressful at times. But in truth this was a gross understatement. The unhealthy food, alcohol, and long work hours were the tip of a toxic workplace iceberg. I was spending my days immersed in the most ruthless and drama-filled culture I would ever experience. Think *Lord of the Flies* in a landscape of cubicles, offices, boardrooms, and happy hours. And it had been a roller-coaster ride. We had grown the company at a torrid pace, only to have it fall off a cliff and shrink back down after the stock market crashed, and now we were building it back up all over again. As the VP who oversaw the company's largest department, I had to let dozens of people go during our downsizings, and many of these people were my friends. In one case I had to meet with an employee at his home because he was out on paternity leave helping to care for his newborn. This individual was a personal friend I had recruited away from a stable job just a few months earlier. In total I laid off more than fifty people, and the entire experience had taken a substantial toll on me, mentally and physically.

I returned my attention to the doctor as he went on to explain that pericarditis was an inflammation of the lining around the heart, and that most cases are mild and improved on their own, though he recommended treating it with a course of anti-inflammatories and keeping a close eye on it.

His diagnosis didn't sound that bad to me, so my hopes rose a little. But I still had some anxiety because something didn't seem right. The doctor's demeanor felt disproportionately serious relative to his findings.

"That's the good news," he said, looking down again at the test results and flipping through them one more time. He hesitated for a moment and seemed to reach a decision. He closed the folder and set it aside. Then he looked me straight in the eyes, and said, "Your test results are very concerning. If you don't make some major changes, you're going to be dead before you're forty."

The doctor's message left me dazed and didn't fully sink in until later, well after he walked me through the specific findings and lifestyle changes that he recommended. But his words hit their mark and stuck. I realized that allowing my health to deteriorate to this point had been shortsighted and could have dire consequences not only for me, but for my loved ones as well. I was working myself into an early grave, and I had two adorable kids at home depending on me. Sure, I had begun to build up some savings, but it was paltry when compared to my car loan, home mortgage, and a heaping pile of student debt.

It took a good scare and the blunt words of a concerned physician to pull myself off the path to an early grave and begin my journey toward wellness. A journey that would involve a torrent of changes over the following months and years that were necessary to take care of my body and restore my health. It started with a somewhat drastic but necessary change—I quit my job. I traded in the expensive car for something more modest, rented out our house, left the Washington, DC, area and moved into a log home in the Adirondack Mountains, where I took about six months off to get myself back on track. Day-to-day lifestyle changes that I made over subsequent years include routine exercise, a much improved diet, elimination of alcohol, and a variety of practices to improve both my mental health and the quality of my sleep.

> "When health is absent, wisdom cannot reveal itself,
> art cannot manifest, strength cannot fight, wealth becomes
> useless, and intelligence cannot be applied."
> —*Herophilus*

By taking steps to improve my physical and mental well-being, my goal was to improve my quality of life and extend my health span. By health span, I mean the number of years I have left where my health doesn't preclude me from enjoying life. Yes, of course I'd like to live longer, but I also want to live free from disease and be able to engage in activities that are meaningful to me. Despite my best efforts, I'm not sure I can fully reverse all of the damage I did to myself earlier in life, but I do the best I can. I'm certainly far from perfect, and my efforts to embrace a healthy existence are a journey that continues to this day. Fortunately, I now have the perspective to realize that my self-neglect was a terrible mistake. It ran up a massive bill that almost came due early and in the biggest way—a bill that I've spent the last couple of decades working to pay down.

I am in no way alone in my struggles to make the right decisions with regards to my wellness. In fact, it places me in the majority. Sadly, most of us do more to maintain our vehicles than we do our own bodies. We ensure that our auto receives routine service, proper and adequate fuel, and appropriate fluid levels. We exercise caution when driving and avoid extremes that our vehicle isn't designed to handle. Why do we do these things? Because it's necessary for the vehicles to run properly. And because a failure to do so will shorten the life of our car. How is it that we can't exercise the same level of care for ourselves? If a vehicle dies, it can be replaced. But when it comes to our minds and bodies, our options are a lot more limited.

> "Take care of your body, it's the only place you have to live."
> —*Jim Rohn*

What do you need to do in order to take better care of yourself? You certainly don't have to go to extremes, but extending your health span will entail some basic level of overall wellness, including physical fitness, mental health, proper nutrition, healthy relationships, and adequate rest. Most of us already know what to do, but it can be hard to actually do it. In part, this is because tackling a big change head on through brute force of will is often futile, and just leaves us feeling bad about ourselves. The greatest of aspirations can fall flat if you attempt to undertake too drastic a change at once. We all have a tendency to overestimate what we can accomplish in shorter time frames like a week, month, or year, but we underestimate what we can do over the long haul, like in five, ten, or twenty years. I experienced this the first time I decided to go out for a run in an effort to work off some of that extra weight. I had just moved into the log cabin and was feeling motivated to start my new life. So I laced up my running shoes for the first time in years, thinking I'd go for a quick three miles, but I was less than a half mile in when I nearly passed out from the exertion. Hunched over, knees and lungs screaming, frustrated and embarrassed, I almost gave up. Thankfully, I decided to walk instead. After a few weeks this progressed to alternating between walking and running, and only after many months of steady progress was I able to actually complete a full three miles without stopping. Running became part of my life, and a few years later I'd be running marathons. A decade after that I'd be running ultramarathons. I had a similar experience with my eating. I tried a few fad diets, and each time I failed miserably. But then I decided to make a few small changes, one at a time, over months and years. Undertaking incremental improvements in this manner allowed me to experience small wins early on and build momentum. As a result, many of the improvements stuck. Thanks to the lifestyle changes, I eventually reached and maintained a healthy weight, which has improved both my physical well-being and my state of mind. I feel better about myself, and I'm an overall healthier and happier person.

As these examples illustrate, being patient, taking baby steps, and making changes in moderation are more likely to result in practices that are sustainable long term. And those little things can add up over time and make a big difference. When people ask me how they can improve their health the way I did, I recommend they start with something small and concrete. Incorporating a reasonable level of movement into your daily routine is more likely to yield positive, sustainable results than signing up for a marathon. Make modest commitments and turn them into a habit. Maybe take the stairs instead of the elevator. Go to bed and wake up at the same times. Drink more water. Get thirty minutes of natural light each day. Take walks after dinner instead of watching TV. Put some limits on screen time. It's not always effective to eliminate our indulgences in their entirety, but we should at least strive for moderation. And it takes discipline. Change won't work unless it can be maintained, which requires doing actions often enough that they become deeply ingrained. Eventually the decision-making process goes away, and that's when things get so much easier. That's when we become who we envisioned, and we act like it.

> "Every man is the builder of a temple, called his body . . .
> We are all sculptors and painters, and our material is
> our flesh and blood and bones."
> —*Henry David Thoreau*

Another important strategy I've learned is to think about how I may view the decisions I'm making today in five or ten years. It's a skill I initially learned in the business world but am now able to apply to other areas of my life. There are so many powerful forces at work in our society that incessantly pressure us to sacrifice what's in our long-term best interest at the altar of short-term gratification. And this is especially true with issues surrounding our wellness. Companies spend billions of dollars on research, technology, and advertising in an effort to persuade us that we should indulge in short-term pleasures at the expense of our long-term well-being. Maintaining the clarity and discipline to rebuff these influences is a tall order. Yet that's exactly what we need to do in order to be our best selves.

Whenever I'm struggling to make the right decision, I just ask myself, "Five years from now, if I were to look back, what course of action would I be at peace with? Which decision would I be grateful I made? Which one might I regret?" It's almost always better to do the things that, even if unpleasant in the short term, you'll feel good about later on. The things that are bad for you may feel good in the moment, but they don't usually sit well afterward.

Every step you take to improve your well-being will be worthwhile. There is so much at stake. Your health is directly correlated to your quality of life, and even small improvements will make you feel better and boost performance in every pursuit. Not to mention the fact that even the most modest changes can add years to your life.

For more specific guidance on wellness and extending your health span, I would recommend the *Huberman Lab* podcast, or any content from Dr. Andrew Huberman, a renowned neuroscientist and professor at the Stanford School of Medicine whose advice is deeply rooted in scientific research. Huberman's "Core 5 Pillars of Mental and Physical Health" include a series of critical daily actions: sleep, sunlight, movement, nutrition, and social connection. Another excellent resource is Dan Buettner and his book *The Blue Zones Secrets for Living Longer: Lessons From the Healthiest Places on Earth*. Buettner analyzes the world's five geographic locations and cultures where the highest percentage of residents reach the age of one hundred, delving into the specific practices that these people follow and the unique aspects of their lives that have allowed them to live longer, happier lives. Based on these findings he offers guidance on how we can do the same.

WHAT DO I WANT FOR YOU?

I want you to avoid some of the mistakes I made. To recognize at an earlier age that maintaining your physical and mental well-being is a prerequisite for living life to its fullest and extending your life and health span. Remember that you only get one body—it's the vessel within which you will experience life and bring forth your creations and contributions to the world.

I want you to know that the quality of your life is in large part dependent on how well you take care of yourself—mind, body, and spirit. And to make decisions about your wellness that reflect an appreciation for how precious life is.

I want you to understand the steep price and potentially tragic consequences should you fail to adequately care for yourself. A price that will not only be paid by you, but those who love you, including me, and the rest of the world, which will be robbed of your presence and everything beautiful you would have brought into creation.

I want you to live the longest, happiest, and healthiest life possible.

10

SPIRITUALITY

The Things That Are Unseen

> Spirituality is recognizing and celebrating that we are all inextricably connected to each other by a power greater than all of us and that our connection to that power and to one another is grounded in love and compassion. Practicing spirituality brings a sense of perspective, meaning, and purpose to our lives.
> —*Brené Brown*

> We do not need more intellectual power, we need more spiritual power. We do not need more of the things that are seen, we need more of the things that are unseen.
> —*Calvin Coolidge*

As I entered the monastery's temple, I felt a sense of wonder at the simple beauty and welcoming solitude that emanated from the space within. Its holiness was almost palpable. I was particularly struck by the old, wood-framed windows spanning the walls on either side, framing views of the majestic, snowcapped Himalayas and allowing rich beams of sunshine to enter the space and spread across the floor. Looking closely, you could see minute particles of dust dancing and sparkling in the sun's rays, which gave the temple an even more mystical aura.

We were here to meditate, so I scanned the temple for a place to sit, and felt drawn to a comfortable-looking spot near the rear where the sunlight fell on the floor in a shape formed by the window through which it passed. I walked over and seated myself in the middle of this inviting swath of sunshine, feeling the warmth on my face. I crossed my legs and tucked both feet below the opposite knee, straightened my back, and reverently brought my hands up to a prayer pose in front of me as I had observed others doing. I took a few deep breaths, then closed my eyes and settled in, relaxing and noting that the silence was nearly complete, broken only by the faint sounds of the morning breeze outside, the occasional crowing of a distant rooster, or the slow, soft steps of others entering and leaving the temple. I had practiced meditation on and off for the past few years, but in this peaceful moment it felt more natural and comfortable. Like this was where I was supposed to be right now, and this was what I was supposed to be doing.

After a short time, my thoughts began to clear, a calm began to fill me, and I felt lighter, like a weight was being slowly and gently lifted from me. And then I felt free. Free of all the stress and turmoil that incessantly plagues my mind. Free of any expectations, insecurities, or judgment. Instead, I felt feelings of peace, gratitude, and love. I experienced the sensation of being outside of myself, and I felt somehow more connected to this magical and sacred place. In one way, it didn't feel real, and in another, it felt more real than anything.

Eventually, my thoughts returned, and I realized that I couldn't feel the sunlight anymore. I slowly opened my eyes and was surprised to see that the sun had already risen enough to shift the angle by which it was passing through the window, and I was no longer within the boundary of its rays. I didn't think I had been meditating for long, but clearly more time had passed than I realized. This wasn't consistent with my prior experiences with meditation. I have a monkey mind that tends to run rampant, so quieting it for an extended period of time was a struggle—ten minutes of stillness could feel like an eternity. But the temple seemed to instill tranquility, and meditation came more naturally. Instead of wrestling with my mind as I usually did, I just let it go, and it naturally went to a place of serenity.

The level of peace and calm I felt on that day, combined with the simple beauty and sanctity of the setting, made my visit to that temple in Nepal unlike anything I had experienced before. In addition to the gift of the moment itself, the experience offered a glimpse of what could lie ahead if I continued on my spiritual journey. It provided me with a sense of direction and certainty that I was walking the right path.

One of the things I appreciate about spirituality is that it's such a broad and inclusive concept that is open to wide interpretation. Yes, there are some commonly recurring themes, but spirituality can hold a space unique to each of us, and our interpretations of the term may change as we evolve on our own spiritual voyage. While these aspects of spirituality can make it seem more nebulous, I think they're important to mention in the context of this book, because I have no desire or intent to represent myself as an expert, guru, or some kind of master spiritualist, if such a person exists. What I share here are my own humble reflections on spirituality and what it means to me, offered for the benefit of your consideration and contemplation.

A common misconception is that spirituality is the same as religion. While I think most would agree that religious faith falls under the umbrella of spirituality, religions tend to be constrained within more rigid bounds. Religious beliefs and rituals are generally more well-documented, structured, and practiced in groups, while spirituality is more inward-focused and personal-growth oriented, which I like. The more intimate and freer nature of spirituality appeals not only to me, but to many others as well. In an article published by the *Atlantic*, journalist Caroline Kitchener reported that:

Americans are leaving organized religion in droves: they disagree with their churches on political issues; they feel restricted by dogma; they're deserting formal organizations of all kinds. Instead of atheism, however, they're moving toward an identity captured by the term "spirituality." Approximately sixty-four million Americans—one in five—identify as "spiritual but not religious."

Despite reported trends, I think it's important to acknowledge that spirituality and religion do not need to be mutually exclusive, and it's very common for followers of a specific religious order to embark on a parallel journey of spiritual growth and enlightenment. In fact, there are even more people who identify as "spiritual *and* religious" (nearly one in three Americans) than people who identify as "spiritual and *not* religious."[2]

My personal experience with religion followed a path not unlike so many others who have become disillusioned. I was raised Roman Catholic, but parts of the doctrines never felt quite right, and by the time I finished high school I found it difficult to reconcile the virtues espoused from the pulpit with the disturbing and widespread scandals being exposed, one of which struck too close to home. In my senior year of high school, it was revealed that our parish priest, who I had grown to trust, had been accused of sexually abusing an altar boy, and additional allegations would follow. The news left me feeling both disgusted and betrayed. The apparent hypocrisy of the Church not only prompted me to abandon Catholicism, but also left me feeling jaded about religion in general. I felt little motivation to contemplate the existence or nature of God, though I remained open to the presence of a higher power.

My interest in spirituality emerged later in life, though I didn't initially identify it as such or set out on an intentional path. In many ways, it blossomed in parallel with some of my greater professional achievements. As the accolades rolled in and my net worth soared, those external trappings gave me less and less satisfaction. The goalposts were constantly moving, and I was chasing things that were ephemeral. Things that would never be enough. I learned firsthand that money, possessions, and status are too superficial to provide real fulfillment. Any pleasure derived from such things is fleeting, and trying to sustain it is like grasping at the wind.

When my old dreams and accomplishments began to feel increasingly shallow, I was left feeling adrift. But I also knew there must be more. So I turned inward, redirecting my energies toward working on myself. Time I had previously dedicated to professional pursuits increasingly shifted to personal growth and development, and the change felt right. I became more introspective, and I realized that seeking happiness outside of myself was a fool's game. To be genuinely happy I needed to know who I really was and to live a life in closer alignment. And I had to do a better job of grounding myself. To quiet my mind, regulate my emotions, and find some level of peace amidst internal turmoil and the chaos of the world around me. I committed to being more present and embracing gratitude, while exploring practices like meditation, journaling, and yoga. These aspirations prompted me to voraciously consume books, podcasts, and other content that provided clarity and nurtured a rising interest in spiritual growth—an interest that was further nourished and eventually elevated to a conviction during my time in Nepal.

The pursuit of spiritual growth is now a meaningful part of my life. Yet when people ask me what I mean by spirituality, I find there's no simple answer. Even though spirituality is becoming more mainstream, it still raises questions. And it's challenging to explain such a big concept and something so deeply personal without trivializing it or sounding too philosophical or preachy. Any explanation invariably falls short. But it is arguably one of the most important concepts or lessons I can share with you, and this book would not be complete without it, regardless of whether I can do it justice.

All that said, what spirituality means to me right now could best be boiled down to three key elements.

1 – Self-Discovery

First and foremost, my spirituality involves exploring and becoming my true self. For me, this is a process that involves the examination and unpacking of life experiences and becoming aware of the effects they've had, something that I have done both independently and with the help of a therapist. Achieving this consciousness is not easy. As I touched on in Chapters 1 and 7, it requires us to untangle our authentic selves from all those parts that have emerged in response to harmful influences, both internal and external. To embrace our true identity and lean into what brings us energy and peace, while letting go of what doesn't serve us. I've made the mistake of wasting too many minutes, hours, and years fighting inner battles that stem from being misaligned with who I really am. As modern philosopher Deepak Chopra said, "Awakening is not changing who you are, but discarding who you are not."

"Who looks outside, dreams; who looks inside, awakes."
—*Carl Jung*

I also learned that an important spiritual aspect of self-discovery is getting out of our own heads. Recognizing that our thoughts and emotions are transient mental phenomena that are not who we really are. This concept, that we are not the voices in our heads but instead the observer of those voices, able to exert influence over them, is by no means new or novel in any respect. The concept is explored in depth by modern books such as *The Power of Now* and *The Untethered Soul*, but it's also present in various forms within early philosophies and sacred texts, perhaps most notably within the Upanishads—ancient Vedic Sanskrit writings that supplied the basis of later Hindu philosophy and laid the foundation for the Bhagavad Gita, which is one of the most revered texts in human history. Even though the Bhagavad Gita was written three thousand years ago, its teachings underpin many modern-day spiritual practices.

My experience in Nepal inspired me to learn more about these texts and prioritize meditation, which has emerged as one of the primary methods I employ for both quieting my mind and connecting with my true self. While there are many different types of meditation that people find beneficial, and we all need to follow our own path, I have elected to practice Transcendental Meditation (TM), a widely adopted, nondenominational technique that was developed by Maharishi Mahesh Yogi, who gained fame as the spiritual advisor to the Beatles and is widely credited for bringing meditation to the West. Even though TM is rooted in ancient Vedic tradition, and Maharishi was a Hindu monk, the technique's popularity can largely be attributed to its science and evidence-based approach. In addition to TM, I sometimes also practice Metta, a traditional Buddhist meditation focused on loving-kindness that has been around for thousands of years. You can find a wide variety of Metta and other guided meditation practices on platforms and apps such as Insight Timer, Headspace, or YouTube.

2 – Becoming My Best Self

Meditation has also helped with the second area of focus in my own spirituality, which is a commitment to self-actualization, or achieving my full potential by elevating myself to a higher level of being. To replace stress and anxiety with an inner peace. To find my center of gravity and open up my mind and my heart. To love myself and others. To cast aside any baser instincts such as hostility or selfishness and be a person who embodies virtues such as peace, kindness, compassion, and generosity, and to manifest these in the world around me. To be my best self.

> "The spiritual journey is not about becoming better than anyone else, but becoming better than your previous self."
> —*The Fourteenth Dalai Lama*

Toward this goal, I am learning to do a better job of living life with more intention—staying present, heightening my senses, and achieving a greater awareness of, appreciation for, and connectedness to others and the world around me. In the words of poet W. B. Yeats, "The world is full of magic things, patiently waiting for our senses to grow sharper."

The Upanishads challenge us to go even further, looking beyond our senses. As spiritual teacher and author Eknath Easwaran explained, "It is unreasonable to suppose that there is no more to reality than the senses of one species on one small planet can perceive. Unless we truly believe that nothing is real except what our senses register, we must accept that there is more 'out there' than what we see, hear, taste, and smell."

3 – A Higher Power

The third element of my spiritual focus involves not only opening myself up to things that are beyond the limits of our ability to see, but also to a deeper sense of purpose and the presence of a higher power. I don't believe the specifics of what this higher power is, or the form it takes, is as important as the fact that there is something beyond us, and in my opinion such matters are worthy of exploration.

Some faiths revolve around divine, celestial, or supreme beings. Others lean toward a more metaphysical presence that might manifest itself in the form of the universe itself, energy, vibrational frequencies, or even love. Or combinations of all of the above. From a spiritual point of view, I believe there are valuable insights to be gleaned and goodness to be found in all the major faiths. In fact, strip away the dogma and the world's most established religions are more aligned than disparate. Musician and activist John Lennon expressed a similar point of view: "I believe in God, but not as one thing, not as an old man in the sky. I believe that what people call God is something in all of us. I believe that what Jesus and Mohammed and

Buddha and all the rest said was right. It's just that the translations have gone wrong."

My openness to the presence of things beyond us and a higher power may have been influenced by my early exposure to religion, but it's more deeply rooted in life experiences. There are just too many profound occurrences in life that cannot be explained beyond some kind of greater influence or divine intervention. How many times have you had something happen that goes too far beyond coincidence or logic to rationalize? When maybe you feel guided by the universe or led by the hand of God? I think there is a tendency for such experiences to make us uncomfortable enough to just set them aside—to leave them unexamined and move on with our lives. But, as we will explore in Chapter 14, miracles are all around us—some that just can't be ignored and others that are more easily overlooked or even buried in the mundane. You just need to be open, and to look.

The last thing I would say about my own spirituality is that I view it as an evolutionary process—more of a life journey than an actual destination. To borrow from Buddhism, it is a path to enlightenment, which in my opinion is worth striving for, even if such a level of transcendence should ultimately prove unattainable.

WHAT DO I WANT FOR YOU?

I want you to give deliberate thought to your own beliefs and spirituality. To be open to different faiths and practices, including meditation. To explore and know your true self. To feel a deeper connection to the people and life around you, and to consider the existence of things outside of what you experience with your five senses. I want you to be able to see the world in a different light and not to rule out the possibility of things existing beyond yourself and the material realm.

I want you to be respectful of all faiths, to recognize the good in them, and not cast judgment. I want you to feel complete freedom to explore and embrace any aspects of spirituality that might resonate with you. To approach spirituality on your own terms, but with an open heart and curiosity. To embody the type of person that the Bhagavad Gita calls *jijnasu*, or "those with a passion to know."

And should you elect to do so, I want you to experience the deep peace and meaningful benefits that introducing and embracing elements of spirituality can bring to your life. To open yourself to the possibility of experiencing transcendent moments like I did in Nepal. To be as the proverbial lotus flower that emerges through the muddy water in your own garden, and blossoms into something of radiant beauty.

11

EMPATHY

The Essence of Our Humanity

> Could a greater miracle take place than for us to look through each other's eye for an instant?
> —*Henry David Thoreau*

> Be kind, for everyone you meet is fighting a hard battle.
> —*Plato*

When I first met Luisa, it was evening and she was seated at the kitchen table of her home in Bajos de Haina, a city in the Dominican Republic where I was living and, at the age of twenty-six, serving as a Peace Corps volunteer. Luisa was hunched over a textbook and doing calculations in her binder. The kitchen was small and crude, lit by a dim, bare light bulb hanging from an extension cord, and Luisa had to squint to see her work. She was tired and frustrated—struggling with a math problem and anxious to complete her assignment before she had to leave for work.

Luisa was two years older than me, and for the past ten years she had been taking one college course at a time in nearby Santo Domingo, desperately trying to make a better life for herself and her family. She was nearly two-thirds of the way to earning an engineering degree, but her life was a grind. Paying tuition required her to hold two full-time jobs. She would work the day shift at a local factory, getting off in time to study and attend class, and then head to a second factory, where she worked the night shift. One job wasn't enough to cover her expenses, and the employers wouldn't allow double shifts because the hazardous work environment proved too dangerous if you weren't alert. Luisa's workaround was to hold two jobs.

Luisa's younger sister, whom I had met and befriended through my volunteer work, made a great production of introducing me to Luisa as "Engineer Brian Murray from the United States of America" and proceeded to tell her sister with obvious pride what degrees I held, all of which made me squirm with embarrassment. After we exchanged brief pleasantries, Luisa politely excused herself, explaining that she was having a difficult time with her math assignment and needed to finish her work. That's when her sister excitedly suggested that I help and, happy to assist, I sat down at the small table with Luisa, studied the homework problem, and carefully reviewed her calculations. What I was seeing made me swallow hard, as a feeling of deep embarrassment rose within me. The problem was extremely complex, as was the work Luisa had already done. And I couldn't understand it. I reviewed everything and tried my best, but I couldn't help her. It was too advanced.

It's not like I didn't have math skills. I had recently earned a masters of engineering from the Johns Hopkins University, and I was a licensed professional engineer. Yet here I was in a tiny kitchen with a tin roof and dirt floor, trying to help someone who had attended an appallingly underfunded and understaffed high school in a developing country. Someone who could only afford to take one college course at a time by working two horrific jobs. Yet she was doing math problems that were beyond my comprehension. I was embarrassed that I couldn't solve the problem, but I was also ashamed because of the assumptions I had made about Luisa. Based on where she lived, I had expected the math she was doing to be simple. But I now realized that, given the opportunity, Luisa could probably hold her own at any engineering program in the world.

Afterward, standing outside of the small, tin shack that Luisa called home, I took everything in. The one-bedroom house was so tiny, yet she shared it with her mother and sister. Similar homes were tightly packed for as far as I could see, connected by a maze of narrow dirt roads that were riddled with potholes and open sewage ditches. With each inhalation, you could smell a combination of cooking food, raw sewage, and acrid smoke from the industrial zone that was a stone's throw away. Bajos de Haina is considered one of the most polluted places on earth and has been referred to as the "Dominican Chernobyl." According to the United Nations, its inhabitants have the highest levels of lead contamination in the world. The number of health problems and birth defects I observed while living there backed this up. In that moment of reflection, I was profoundly saddened. Life is a gift, but it can sometimes be terribly cruel and unfair.

There was a shift that took place inside me that evening. Nothing has ever humbled me more. When my Peace Corps service was over, I would return to the United States with a deeper appreciation and gratitude for the many privileges and bountiful opportunities we enjoy. With a deep resolve to make the most of the advantages afforded to me. And with a new level of empathy, respect, and compassion for people doing incredible things in faraway places under circumstances beyond our comprehension.

Many years later, while working as a professor, I would get a harsh reminder that there are plenty of people in our own communities who face great hardship as well. And that it's a mistake to assume you know what's going on in other people's lives.

Five minutes into delivering my lecture, I was annoyed to see one of my students arrive late, amble over to her seat, and collapse in her chair. Emily was an enigma to me, as were many of my students. It was my first semester teaching business classes at a community college, and I was disappointed by the lack of commitment and effort that seemed to run rampant among the student body. From what I could discern, Emily was a kind, intelligent, and charismatic young woman, but it seemed like she didn't have her priorities in order—not only was her punctuality suspect, but she frequently appeared tired and distracted, and the quality of her work was inconsistent. She was clearly not working up to her potential. And as I continued the lecture, I grew increasingly irritated. Emily was speaking with her friend in a low voice, and she proceeded to put her head face down on her desk. I speculated that she had been partying the night before and was now dealing with a hangover. I found Emily's behavior disrespectful, so when class ended, I asked her to stay after so I could speak with her.

Emily remained in her seat as her classmates filed out of the room. She sat up but kept her head bowed. Her long, curly hair blocked her face as I began to speak in a stern voice and share my disappointment. Her demeanor struck me as insolent, which only further incited me. "Can you please look at me when I'm speaking to you?" I asked frustratedly. She slowly lifted her head, and her hair parted enough for me to see that Emily's normally bright eyes were dull, red, and puffy. For the first time, I also realized how disheveled she looked. And when she finally made eye contact with me, she immediately started trembling and burst into tears.

It turned out that Emily was being severely abused by her stepfather. The prior evening things had taken a turn for the worse. He had dragged her out of the house and into the woods, where he showed her that he had dug a grave, which she described in hauntingly vivid detail. It was about eight feet long, four feet wide, and a full six feet deep with sheer sides. Her stepfather shoved Emily into the grave, told her to lie down, and threatened that if she called for help or tried to get out, he would bury her alive. And that's where she spent the night, curled up in a grave, smelling freshly dug earth, nearly hypothermic, and too afraid to move until her stepfather left for work that morning. After he left, she was able to grab onto some roots and climb out, and then she showered, changed, and drove to school as quickly as possible, completely exhausted. She apologized for being late, which nearly broke my heart.

I was horrified by what I learned, but managed to keep my composure and comforted Emily as best I could. I encouraged her to call the police, walked her to one of the campus counselor's offices, and made sure she got professional support and guidance. I felt a deep empathy and compassion for her situation, but I was also angry. Emily was such a kind person, and it just seemed so *wrong*. Afterward, I would chastise myself for getting irritated with her, and spend time reflecting on how dangerous it was to make assumptions or judge people. Sometimes the stories we tell ourselves are entirely inaccurate. It certainly wasn't the first time I'd made such a mistake. A decade had passed since my Peace Corps service, and I still hadn't learned my lesson. I vowed to do better. This was a personal commitment that served me well moving forward, both during my tenure as a professor and in my life afterward.

My work as a Peace Corps volunteer and community college professor put me in close contact with diverse groups of people, and some of the hardships I witnessed were just brutal. During my time in the Dominican Republic, I also visited the neighboring country of Haiti, the poorest nation in the Western Hemisphere, where I beheld conditions that were nearly incomprehensible. Half of this country's population lives on less than one dollar per day. Living and traveling in underdeveloped countries helped me to accept the hard truth that a disturbingly high percentage of the earth's population lives in poverty and substandard conditions, and that simply by being born in a developed country, we're more privileged and have opportunities unavailable to most. And the nine years I spent as a college professor showed me that you don't need to travel abroad to find good people who are suffering or facing adversity. They can be found in every community. These experiences afforded me an invaluable opportunity to put things in better perspective, cultivate humility, and foster a deeper sense of empathy for others.

> "Yet, taught by time, my heart has learned to glow
> for other's good, and melt at other's woe."
> —*Homer*

While some of my experiences and the hardships I witnessed in these environments may have hit me like a physical blow, I've also learned a very important lesson: you don't need to go anywhere special to know in your heart that everyone is fighting their own battles, and it's never a good idea to cast judgment. A person doesn't need to be impoverished or lying in a freshly dug grave to suffer intensely. We all face challenges and situations that are real and can cut deeply, even if on their surface such hardships may appear more pedestrian or otherwise not merit empathy or compassion. Believing that you can make judgments and draw accurate conclusions based on someone's external circumstances is folly because a person's window dressing rarely reflects what they have experienced or their internal state of affairs. Some of the most tormented people I've met are wealthy and portray an outward image of having a perfect life. Such a person might not seem like they should merit empathy or compassion. But dig a little deeper and you may find that they carry the pain of deep wounds, often as a result of childhood trauma or mental illness. So instead of judging or harboring preconceptions, I try as hard as possible to have grace and be empathetic—to put myself in another person's shoes. And when I don't know enough to imagine what it must be like for them, I try to remind myself that I don't know their circumstances. To exercise patience and give them the benefit of the doubt.

> "Have compassion and empathy in your heart. Many people are suffering deep emotional anguish beneath the surface of their lives, and smile even as they hurt inside."
> —*Jim Palmer*

Embracing empathy in this manner is a lot easier in concept than in practice, and though I'm now operating from a higher level of awareness and doing a better job, I'm far from perfect. This is particularly true when someone says or does something antithetical to my personal values, or causes harm to myself or someone I care about. Feeling empathy toward someone in this situation and maintaining our own equanimity is an undeniably tall order, and requires an almost transcendent level of groundedness. But it's certainly worth striving for.

It's also innately more challenging to be empathetic when confronted with someone who seems so entirely unrelatable or different from us. Someone who falls outside of our mental framework of what's normal or acceptable. As humans, we have a survival mechanism that perceives anything unfamiliar as threatening and can trigger base instincts such as fear, which blocks empathy and can prompt defensiveness and judgment. When faced with such situations, I try to acknowledge my feelings but then consciously tell myself to let them go and to not judge, make assumptions, or be defensive. The same applies when someone does or says something that upsets me. A strategy that I've found useful is to create hypothetical scenarios in my mind around what types of circumstances an individual may have had to contend with or what things they might be dealing with right now, giving them the most generous reason I can think of for their behavior. And I try my best not to take anything too personally. As Don Miguel Ruiz shares in *The Four Agreements*, how someone speaks or acts toward us is invariably more a reflection of what's going on in their internal world than it is about us. Embracing this premise as truth, while not easy, can help us take a lot less to heart and maintain a higher level of empathy for others.

It can also be difficult to summon up empathy for people or populations that are distant or faceless. Suffering is just a lot harder to ignore when you know and care about the people dealing with it, a factor that heightened the impact of my years of teaching and Peace Corps service—I grew to know and care about some of the people affected, which broke down barriers. Their hardship hit closer to home and felt more real, which heightened my sensitivity and emotions. Faced with such situations, even the most cynical among us are inclined to feel empathetic. But the world is infinitely broader than our own circles. We all need to remember that just because someone is far away and we don't know them doesn't make them any less human, and the pain they feel isn't any less real. Like us, they have family, friends, hopes, and dreams.

Despite how challenging it can be to practice empathy, I believe it is well worth the effort and is a critical skill to embrace in our everyday lives. Being empathetic is good for our overall well-being. Among other things, it fosters more and deeper connections with the people around us, which leads to more happiness. Empathy allows us to better understand others and improves our interpersonal skills. To be better colleagues, leaders, friends, siblings, parents, or partners. Being empathetic also facilitates forgiveness and contributes to our peace of mind. But most importantly, empathy is at the root of what makes us human. Of what unites us and makes us kind and good as a species. Empathy is what ignites compassion, which is the drive to make a difference. To help alleviate suffering and improve the circumstances of others, which is something we should all aspire to do.

> "The nature of humanity, its essence, is to feel another's pain as one's own, and to act to take that pain away. There is a nobility in compassion, a beauty in empathy, a grace in forgiveness."
> —*John Connolly*

WHAT DO I WANT FOR YOU?

I want you to make your best effort to be empathetic. To imagine what it might be like to walk in other people's shoes. To see the world through their eyes, and feel what they feel. And when you don't have enough knowledge or information to relate, to accept the limits of your own perspective and remind yourself that everyone faces challenges and hardships.

I want you to stay humble and strive to have empathy for all humans, even if they are distant or faceless. To marshal the strength of will to suppress your innate fear of people, practices, and viewpoints that are different or unfamiliar. To try not to take things too personally, be judgmental, or make assumptions.

I want you to steadily work toward making empathy a default. To embrace it, express it openly, and weigh it in your decisions. To make empathy a habit so it will become a part of your character.

Achieving this level of clarity is a lofty goal, but worth the effort. So I hope you will lean into your empathy and nurture it, allowing it to blossom into compassion, which will provide you with the desire and motivation to help. To do acts of kindness, lift up those around you, and use your gifts to make a positive difference in the world.

12

GENEROSITY

The Selfless Virtue

> We make a living by what we get, but we make a life by what we give.
> —*Winston Churchill*

> When you work to improve the lives of others, you indirectly elevate your own life in the process. When you take care to practice random acts of kindness daily, your own life becomes far richer and more meaningful. To cultivate the sacredness and sanctity of each day, serve others in some way.
> —*Robin Sharma*

As I looked ahead toward the next house, I saw that it was similar to most of the others we had visited so far—a small, simple structure with open windows and a tin roof. We were in one of the poorest neighborhoods of Bajos de Haina in the Dominican Republic, going door-to-door in an effort to help implement a new waste management plan. It was 1995, and I was now over a year into my service as a Peace Corps volunteer.

Located to the immediate west of Santo Domingo, the city of Haina had a rapidly growing population of just over one hundred thousand and was a hub of industrial activity, home to five electric plants, three large industrial zones, the nation's primary commercial port, and its only gas and oil refineries. Most of Haina's residential areas were highly impoverished, contaminated, and lacked basic services such as potable water, latrines, and trash collection.

In an effort to address one of the greatest areas of need, I had worked with the local government and a consortium of nonprofit organizations to develop a new garbage collection and recycling program. But we quickly realized that such a program could never be successful without some education. My Dominican counterparts pointed out that many of the city's inhabitants considered leaves or shoots of grass in their yards to be trash, and most households would burn plastics and other noxious material, resulting in the inhalation of toxins. Recycling wouldn't work unless individuals could differentiate between organic and inorganic materials and understand how things could be safely disposed of. Since there was no effective way to reach everyone through advertising, I created an educational pamphlet. But many of the residents couldn't read, and the concepts were too complicated to explain with illustrations. Furthermore, it wasn't realistic to expect a pamphlet to change long-held beliefs. So I had decided to take a more direct approach—sitting down with as many people as possible and reviewing the pamphlet in person. To accomplish this, I organized a group of local volunteers, paired people up in teams, and we started the lengthy process of going door-to-door.

As my volunteer companion and I drew closer to the next home, I saw a woman standing in front of the doorway with a small child at her side. The little boy appeared to be five or six years old, and, like most of the kids his age in that neighborhood, he wore nothing but a well-used pair of shorts. I watched as the woman crouched down, spoke into the youngster's ear, and placed something in his hand before he sped off down the street, pumping his little arms and legs with a purpose, bare feet slapping happily on the mud.

When we approached the home, the woman in the doorway greeted us with a warm and welcoming smile. I noted that she wore a floral print dress that, though faded and threadbare, was also freshly pressed, with signs of mending that reflected meticulous care. Despite living in the most trying conditions, most residents showed great pride and attended closely to their homes and appearance. They cherished and cared for their possessions with an attentiveness rarely found among those more privileged. The woman politely listened to my introduction, and graciously invited us into her home so we could sit and talk.

We sat down in her small, sparsely furnished living area and began to explain the program we were working on, presenting her with a copy of the brochure. And that's when the little boy returned, bursting through the front door, out of breath, with a bottle of Coca-Cola in either hand. The woman smiled broadly, taking the bottles from the boy and presenting them to us with obvious pride. She explained that it was a hot day and she was sure we would be thirsty, so she asked us to please enjoy the refreshments.

I was completely stunned. I knew exactly how much the corner shops charged for a bottle of Coke. It was a luxury, and that money probably could have bought enough rice and beans to feed her family for at least a week. I struggled with what to do. I wanted to ask her to return the bottles, but the caps were already off, and I knew she would be insulted. So I did the only thing I could think of to do in the moment. I thanked her profusely and went out of my way to tell her how delicious it was and what a gracious host she was. While this seemed to please her, and it alleviated some of my stress, I still felt guilty. I wished she hadn't made such a gesture. It was evident that this was not an expense she could afford, and I knew the money could have served a better purpose. When we left, I thanked her all over again and gave her a hug before walking out. I had to stop and collect myself before moving on to the next home. Every once in a great while someone does something so kind and unexpected that it restores your faith in humanity. And this was one of those precious moments.

Over subsequent months we distributed brochures to thousands of homes, though it's debatable how successful the entire initiative was. When we eventually distributed trash cans for people to use, many were promptly sold or repurposed as water storage containers. It was disappointing that the program didn't work as intended, but perhaps using the containers in this manner was meeting a greater need. It's challenging to make a meaningful difference when the problems are so vast and the needs so great, but I tried, both on this project and many others, including the orchestration of Haina's first ever beach cleanup, an initiative that, although it may not have made a deep impact, was uniquely rewarding in the sense that there was a visible and quantifiable outcome: more than three hundred kids collected over eight hundred bags of garbage that day.

While I'm pleased with the work I did overall, it would be wrong to characterize my motivations as purely altruistic. I joined the Peace Corps because I wanted to live abroad and experience another culture. I didn't do it to save the world. And in the end, I probably walked away from the experience with more than I contributed, primarily in the form of personal growth. As a volunteer, I was supposed to be the generous one. But anything I gave was returned to me tenfold by some of the nicest and most giving people I have ever encountered. And my cumulative contributions paled in comparison to the selfless gift I received while distributing pamphlets door-to-door. To this day, I've never witnessed a more sincere and kind act of generosity, and it was motivated by nothing more than a heartfelt desire to be hospitable and offer a cold beverage to a complete stranger on a hot day, regardless of the personal cost.

How much better a world would we live in if everyone was so thoughtful and giving?

I'm grateful that most of my professional endeavors have contributed to the benefit of society in different ways, some more significantly than others. But as with my Peace Corps service, I can't take too much credit because generosity was not the primary motivator. I almost always expected something of significance in return. And outside of work, I did not practice acts of generosity as often as I would have liked—something that I now regret and have since rectified. But on those occasions that I did extend myself, the rewards were plentiful. The universe seemed inclined to see that I was paid back in unexpected ways. And the intrinsic benefits were self-evident. To give and help others feels good. It always brings some level of inner peace.

> "For it is in giving that we receive."
> —*St. Francis of Assisi*

Numerous studies have examined the benefits of generosity and consistently found that it improves both physical and mental health, which shouldn't be surprising. Performing acts of generosity makes us feel better about ourselves and makes us happier, particularly if it comes from a good place. It gets us out of our own heads, shifting our internal focus to those around us. Stress levels are reduced, which not only contributes to an improved state of mind but also improves our physical health. Some studies have shown that it can even extend our lifespan. At a higher level, generosity gives us a greater sense of purpose and makes life more meaningful, a benefit that is priceless.

While such personal rewards are obviously compelling, ideally, they are not the primary motivation. I think that generosity can exist on a spectrum, but that the highest level of generosity is a reflection of not only the act itself, but also the goodness of intention. It is born of a desire to help and make a difference for its own sake, without expecting something in return. Through sacrifices of time, materials, or energy in any form, for the benefit of something or someone beyond yourself. Without ulterior motives. Generosity is a selfless virtue rooted in humility, kindness, and compassion that manifests through the act of giving. And the power that generosity brings forth into the world is derived from the internal world of the giver. When the act originates from a purity of intention, it is imbued with a life of its own. It is felt by the recipient and carries forward an energy that wants to grow and spread in the world. A force that influences and compels others to also do good things. To pay it forward.

> "Miss no single opportunity of making some small sacrifice, here by a smiling look, there by a kindly word; always doing the smallest right and doing it all for love."
> —*St. Thérèse of Lisieux*

There is perhaps no better example than the gift of Coca-Cola that I received. That act of generosity, while on its surface appearing limited in reach, was so pure that it was imbued with a greater power. It touched me profoundly, planting a seed in the garden of my mind that took root and thrived, influencing my behavior over a lifetime. And now the act has been immortalized in this book, where it will hopefully touch you in some small way, and its reach will spread even further into the world. Were the woman who gave me the gift to discover its full impact, I'm sure she would be astounded. We can never know for sure how much an act of kindness may grow and spread beyond what we might imagine.

The opposite is also true. When an act of generosity is clouded by selfish interests or ulterior motives, it's shallower and falls flatter, both for the giver and the recipient. As Michael Ende wrote in *The Neverending Story*, "A person's reason for doing someone a good turn matters as much as the good turn itself." Yes, a tainted gesture can still do great good, but it is not felt the same way, and its potential is diminished. In this way, acts of generosity share a similar paradox with acts of creation—the most impactful attainments are almost always realized when they are not sought.

WHAT DO I WANT FOR YOU?

I want you to deliberately perform acts of generosity. To give of yourself to others, whether it be in the form of volunteering your time, sharing your gifts and abilities, giving monetary donations, or performing random acts of kindness. Even being vulnerable and extending kind words can make more of a difference in the lives of others than you might ever know.

I want you to maintain an awareness of your internal motivations. To embrace the kindness and compassion in your heart and allow that to be what fuels your acts of generosity. To make every effort to keep your ego in check, to make your intentions pure, and to not expect anything in return.

I want you to reap all the rewards that you will naturally derive from bringing pure acts of generosity into the world. To feel good about yourself and the difference you're making.

Finally, I want you to be open to receiving the gifts and kind gestures from others that, while unexpected, will almost always come in return. To receive them with both grace and gratitude. To feel their energy, nurture it within you, and harness it to give more.

13

MORTALITY

The Ephemeral Nature of Life

> You're going to die one day, and none of this is going to matter.
> So enjoy yourself. Do something positive. Project some love.
> Make someone happy. Laugh a little bit. Appreciate the moment.
> And do your work.
> —*Naval Ravikant*

> The world is so exquisite with so much love and moral depth, that there is no reason to deceive ourselves with pretty stories for which there's little good evidence. Far better it seems to me, in our vulnerability, is to look death in the eye and to be grateful every day for the brief but magnificent opportunity that life provides.
> —*Carl Sagan*

It was a bright, sunny Friday morning in 1975 in Saratoga Springs, New York. I was seven years old and playing tag with my second-grade classmates on the playground of St. Peter's Elementary School, blissfully unaware of the tragedy that was unfolding close by, or that my fun was about to be abruptly cut short.

"Everybody, get in line!" shouted one of the teachers. "We need to go back inside. *Immediately.*" My indignation at having our playtime interrupted was somewhat muted by the panic evident in the teacher's voice, so I begrudgingly started making my way toward the playground's exit gate. That's when another teacher rushed by, cradling a little girl in her arms. I noted the fear on the teacher's face. And then I saw the blood. "She must have fallen on the slide," speculated a friend who had seen the same thing. Now we heard sirens in the distance as the teachers frantically corralled us through the exit and marched us back inside.

It wasn't until hours later, after we had resumed classes, that we learned about the deranged man who had taken his firearm and started shooting at us from the upper floor of a nearby apartment building. He hit and wounded two of my classmates before the ensuing standoff with police would end when he turned the gun on himself. The entire episode generated a jumble of emotions and confusion—I really didn't know what to think or how to process it. A part of me knew that I could have been shot and killed, but my young mind didn't know what to do with that information. It was the first time I can remember thinking I could die, but in a strange way it didn't seem real to me—it felt more like I'd been in a movie or on a TV show. There was no counseling provided, and I can't recall receiving any kind of support, other than saying a prayer and receiving vague assurances that everyone would be okay. My sense was that people were uncomfortable talking about it: anxious to move on and pretend it didn't happen. And I felt the same way, so I quickly resumed my daily routine and pushed the entire incident out of my young mind, leaving nothing behind but a lingering sense that life was less predictable and safe than I had thought.

Forty-five years later, the school shooting a vague and distant memory, I sat in my car, waiting at the stoplight, frustrated with the crazy traffic and contemplating the busy day ahead. My musings were interrupted when the light turned green. As I began crossing the intersection, I caught a glimpse to my left of a large, black SUV barreling forward at an alarmingly high speed. I realized that it was on a clear trajectory to run the red light and T-bone me. With only a fraction of a second to react, I banked hard right in an attempt to avoid getting crushed. This maneuver would result in a slightly more angled blow just in front of the driver's seat that would spin me around 360 degrees. In the split second before impact, I had one clear thought: "I'm going to die."

The force of the collision was more powerful and jarring than anything I have experienced and caused complete disorientation. I saw stars and struggled to maintain consciousness. There was a loud ringing in my ears. I felt a cold shot of adrenaline course through my body and rapidly blinked my eyes, but was confused by a fog of thick, swirling smoke, severe stinging in my eyes and throat, and an acrid taste in my mouth. I slowly began to regain my faculties, and panic began to set in. I thought the car was on fire, and behind the ringing in my ears I could hear a loud voice asking if I was okay. As the fog cleared further, I pieced together that an OnStar operator was speaking to me, and that the pungent smoke had been discharged from a ruptured airbag. After a few minutes, I could hear sirens in the distance, and, as the reality of what had just happened set in, I began to shake.

Help soon arrived, and miraculously, even though my car was totaled, I was able to walk away from this accident not only alive but with no physical injuries beyond a bad case of whiplash and some deep bruising. The neck issues would linger, but the mental trauma was more difficult to cope with. I knew with absolute certainty that it was the smallest fraction of a second that made the difference between walking away and getting killed. And it was nothing beyond pure luck, or perhaps fate, that I wasn't paralyzed or otherwise severely injured. Getting my head straight and being comfortable on the roads was a lengthy process. That said, there was clear reason to feel deep gratitude. The experience was a difficult but valuable reminder of how impermanent life is. And the world looked a little different afterward. Time felt more precious. There was also fear, but over time it slowly morphed into acceptance. I realized that I didn't know how much time I had. Nobody does. This recognition motivated me to stop putting things off. To not leave things unsaid and undone. When my time came, I wanted to be at peace.

Whether it's some random shooter, a car accident, a lightning strike, or a coconut dropping from a tree, death can come at any time. While it's not something most of us are inclined to contemplate, we all have brushes with death, be it our own or someone else's. We are painfully aware of some of them, and we remain blissfully ignorant of others. When death takes center stage and can't be ignored, it will often prompt some deep feelings to well up inside of us. Yes, we can experience trauma and grief, sometimes to debilitating extremes. But death, or a close encounter with it, can also prompt us to gain a new and healthier perspective on life. To reach a higher level of clarity and consciousness.

> "Life has more meaning in the face of death."
> —*Robert Greene*

Regrettably, such epiphanies are usually fleeting. We make promises to ourselves that fade as quickly as a shooting star. I'm as guilty of this as anyone. I've made deep commitments to myself at more than one funeral, only to find myself almost immediately back to my old ways. And for most of my life I avoided talking about, or even thinking about, death. It made me uncomfortable. It scared me. Unfortunately, such attitudes are fostered and reinforced within American culture, where the subject of death is widely avoided and even considered taboo. We all prefer to assume we're going to live for eternity. Or at least until we're elderly and spending most of our days in a rocking chair. We're all living in denial. As musician Jim Morrison wrote, "No one here gets out alive."

I had all but completely blocked from my memory the fact that I had lived through a school shooting. Then, a few years ago, my mother gave me a musty old cardboard box filled with crinkly scraps from my youth. I was amused as I pulled items out one at a time. There were old report cards stating that I wasn't working up to my potential, art projects that looked like they had been created by an overcaffeinated monkey, and a host of other blasts from the past. And underneath it all I found an old newspaper, yellowed with age. I pulled it out and unfolded it, curious why it was there. And there on the front page was the story of the school shooting. I felt a chill, and the memories came flooding back. It was like realizing that an old, bad dream was actually real.

In hindsight, my lifelong tendency to block the subject of death out of my mind was a mistake. Only later in life did I become aware of the potential benefits of deliberately contemplating one's mortality and, over time, learning to accept that life is finite and could end at any moment. Such introspection was initially triggered when I had a health scare in my thirties, which I shared in Chapter 9. But it really moved to the forefront and became a driving force after my car accident. Once I embarked on this journey with resolve, I realized two things. First, there were the practical considerations. To say my affairs were not in order would be a gross understatement. I have many complicated investments, and there was too much important information that existed nowhere but in my own head. If I had met an untimely demise, I'd be leaving a big hairy mess behind, and whoever had to untangle it all would be cursing me in my grave. Recognizing my mistake, I buckled down and set to work on rectifying this situation.

Second, and more importantly, contemplating my death changed my priorities and how I thought about many aspects of my life, all for the better. While it's difficult to capture the full range of reflections and consequences, there are three particular realizations that stand out to me.

1 – Open Up and Share

First, coming to terms with my own mortality prompted me to make some concrete changes in how I communicate and relate to people around me—especially those closest to me. I realized that it would help put my mind at ease to be more transparent and expressive. To be more readily willing to tell people how I really feel about them because I don't want to die knowing that meaningful things have been left unsaid. In order to manifest this sentiment, I've had to let go of fears around vulnerability and acknowledge that being guarded and reserved with people I care about is shallow and doesn't serve me when death could be around any corner. In this respect, the experience has been liberating. It played a role in my decision to write this book.

> "The bitterest tears shed over graves are for words left unsaid and deeds left undone."
> —*Harriet Beecher Stowe*

Confronting my mortality also heightened my generosity and prompted me to share more—not just my sentiments but also my possessions. After all, what's the point in accumulating wealth if not to give it away and make a difference? And particularly in the lives of those who are most dear to you. This is what prompted me to put my real estate company in an irrevocable trust for the benefit of my loved ones and charitable organizations. There is no virtue in dying with excesses, and I don't need or want more stuff. I believe it's better to share what you have, and to do it while you're still alive and able to influence where the resources are deployed—giving in a manner best aligned with your values.

2 – Practice Gratitude and Mindfulness

Mortality has reinforced my efforts to embrace gratitude and stay more present. To be more mindful. To see life for the miracle it really is and take everything in. As Oliver Burkeman expresses so eloquently in his thought-provoking book *Four Thousand Weeks*, "If you can hold your attention, however briefly or occasionally, on the sheer astonishingness of being, and on what a small amount of being you get—you may experience a palpable shift in how it feels to be here, right now, alive in the flow of time."

Burkeman captures the essence of how I felt walking away from my car accident. I felt like it was a miracle to be alive, and I was more grateful than ever for each and every day. When I had experienced such sentiments in the past, they were more fleeting. But making deliberate efforts to contemplate and accept my own mortality has elevated my conviction to retain these positive feelings and experience their benefits in everyday life—something we explored in more depth in Chapter 8 and will expand on further in Chapter 14.

> "When you arise in the morning, think of what a precious privilege it is to be alive—to breathe, to think, to enjoy, to love."
> —*Marcus Aurelius*

3 – Live a Life of Abundance

Finally, facing and accepting my mortality motivated me to make the most of my time here. To challenge myself, be a better human, and lean into things that are meaningful to me, even if they're not comfortable. Not to put off the experiences or adventures I've always dreamed of. Life is short and precious, so I should honor the privilege of being here by fully savoring my experiences and living life to the fullest.

In his book *Die with Zero*, author Bill Perkins expresses similar sentiments:

> Rather than just focusing on saving up for a big pot full of money that you will most likely not be able to spend in your lifetime, live your life to the fullest now: Chase memorable life experiences, give money to your kids when they can best use it, donate money to charity while you're still alive. That's the way to live life. Remember: In the end, the business of life is the acquisition of memories. So what are you waiting for?

While these realizations may be compelling, growing up in a society where death is feared can make contemplating such things unsettling. It's important to keep thoughts of death in balance and not be consumed by them because too much of a preoccupation with death can fuel anxiety and inhibit your ability to enjoy life. The goal of contemplating death and accepting your mortality is to do the exact opposite—to banish your fear and thereby free yourself up to savor and appreciate the life we are so blessed to experience, regardless of how much time we may or may not have left. Unfortunately, this is much easier said than done. Accepting anything outside of your control is difficult. The thoughts in our heads can run rampant, so it's challenging to strike the right balance between contemplating mortality and becoming overly fixated on it. It helps to stay as mindful and present as possible, which we will address in the next chapter.

"Those who are afraid of death will carry it on their shoulders."
—*Federico García Lorca*

After my car accident, I became concerned I was dwelling on the subject of my death too much. But this concern was rooted squarely within the same mental framework that had suppressed thoughts of death for most of my life. I eventually realized that the gauge I was using to measure the acceptability of such thoughts had been calibrated by the culture of our society, and this scale isn't necessarily aligned with my best interests. I also realized I needed to give myself more grace and learn to accept and even embrace the things I couldn't control. I consoled myself with the recognition that my thoughts and fears had not risen to a level that was preventing me from doing the things I wanted to do and living a full life. In fact, it was having the opposite effect—I was beginning to take actions that I had been too uncomfortable with in the past, and that was a positive thing. These realizations brought me some measure of peace.

Not all societies and cultures share our fear of death. The wisdom of meditating on your own mortality dates back to ancient Rome and is a core tenet of Stoic philosophy. The notion was embraced by ancient philosophers such as Socrates, who called death "the greatest of all human blessings." The benefits of reflecting on mortality are also present in the roots of Buddhism, Judaism, and Christianity. In fact, many ancient texts include references to embracing mortality, and early faith-based statues and artwork incorporate depictions of human skulls as a reminder of our impermanence. The Latin phrase associated with this sentiment is *memento mori*, which roughly translates to "Remember you must die." There are many valuable lessons that can be taken from these and other schools of thought. Ultimately, we are all free to view death through any lens we choose. But acceptance and even taking a positive view of your mortality can foster tranquility and be an impetus for meaningful change. This is what it did for me in the aftermath of my car accident, and what I hope it can do for you.

WHAT DO I WANT FOR YOU?

I want you to cast aside any fears and recognize death for what it is—an inevitable part of life. To acknowledge the finitude of your own life and that of others. To contemplate the reality of your own mortality and harness it as a motivation to embrace gratitude and lead a richer life.

I want you to recognize the extent to which your attitudes and anxieties around death have been influenced by the prevailing attitudes of American culture but know that the world's most prolific faiths and ancient philosophies have advocated a more enlightened perspective. I want you to free yourself to contemplate your mortality in a healthier way.

By embracing the ephemeral nature of life, I want you to be able to say, do, and think about things in a more meaningful way. To achieve a level of consciousness that will allow you to experience life to its fullest. So that when your time comes, you can look back at your life with a sense of fulfillment and without regrets.

14

MINDFULNESS

The Miracles All around Us

> The world is incomprehensibly beautiful,
> an endless prospect of magic and wonder.
> —*Ansel Adams*

> Do not dwell in the past, do not dream of the future,
> concentrate the mind on the present moment.
> —*Buddha*

As I hiked along the Mountains-to-Sea Trail in western North Carolina, I saw another stream crossing ahead. It was a warm Friday afternoon in April 2023, and, after navigating a difficult week, I had decided to reward myself with a long walk in the woods. The trail's stream crossings were beautiful, especially in spring, when the runoff brought the areas around it into brilliant green life faster than the rest of the forest, which was still awakening from winter. The stream I now approached was particularly striking. The water took different paths, breaking apart into multiple rivulets and coming back together, creating a maze of small islands and waterfalls along its descent. On a whim, I diverted from the trail and began to follow the stream uphill, farther and farther into the woods.

I eventually encountered an area where the terrain opened up a bit and three small, cascading waterfalls fell together into a round pool, surrounded by rocks and blooming plants. The natural formations and bright shades of green made the spot feel like an oasis. I found a comfortable place to sit by the pool of water and breathed a deep sigh. Being here, surrounded by the beauty of nature, a weight was lifted from my soul. Everything felt lighter. The sound of birds and the trickling stream were soothing and, as the water flowed past me, it seemed to carry my troubles away with it.

I began to look around me with interest. To *really look*. The way the small stream split three ways and then spilled back together into the same pool was extraordinary. The water was dark but clear, and its surface glittered with reflections of the sunlight and surroundings. Bunches of ferns and broadleaf plants were sprouting everywhere in a variety of patterns, hues, and combinations that were more perfect in their naturalness than any landscaper could ever hope to replicate. The rocks were covered with a carpet of rich, soft, green moss, and ornate mushrooms sprouted from a decaying log. A flicker of movement caught my eye—two butterflies, fluttering and dancing around each other as they passed by on their journey deeper into the forest.

I turned around and saw the sun behind me, sparkling through the budding leaves and swaying branches. I stared with wonder at the hillside behind me, which was sprinkled with flowers: red and white trilliums, wood anemones, and purple columbines, gently swaying in concert with the breeze.

I glanced at the forest floor where I was seated, then curiously reached down with my left hand and grabbed a large handful of the matted, damp, brown leaves. As I began to peel them back, a small salamander darted out the side, froze for a few seconds with his head tilted at an angle, then scurried under more leaves, displeased with my intrusion. I dug a bit deeper and pulled enough leaves back to expose the dark earth below. A worm snapped back down into his hole, and a small centipede with yellow dots on its legs scampered for cover. What was left behind was an elaborate labyrinth of holes and passageways, reflecting a whole underground world rife with activity. I stared in wonder, breathing in the rich, organic smell of the soil and decaying leaves.

There were miracles all around me. It felt almost magical.

For much of my life, I didn't appreciate the sanctity of simple moments like this one. Of being truly mindful, and soaking it all in. But not today. This was a beautiful day.

The gangly young calf was a bit skittish, but after a few minutes of my gentle caresses and soothing tone, Winston quickly warmed up to me. Despite his size, he was just an infant, and his innate craving for affection readily surfaced—he leaned into me, almost losing his fragile balance, stretching his neck out so that I could rub it, showing vulnerability and trust despite having endured a rough start to life at the hands of other humans.

It was a bright and sunny December afternoon in Waynesville, North Carolina. I had recently returned from my trip to Nepal and was doing one of my favorite things—visiting my daughter Alexa at her animal sanctuary, Friendly Fields Farm. Winston was Alexa's most recent rescue. Separated from his mother shortly after birth, he had arrived at the sanctuary sick, exhausted, and severely dehydrated. Deprived of the antibodies he would have received from his mother's milk, Winston was struggling with health issues and was in a tenuous state. But that didn't stop him from being playful and curious or enjoying the company of visitors.

As I rubbed Winston's neck, I felt a sense of calmness and peace. At that moment, there were no thoughts of anything else in the world. Not the past. Not the future. I was wholly immersed in the present, mindful of the sun's warmth, the gentle breeze, the scent of the grass, and most of all this close interaction with one of God's fellow creatures. And I was happy. For as long as I can remember I have loved animals. In part, I think it's because there's a purity there. Animals are not complicated. They don't have agendas. They are authentic. They are just *themselves*. And they are also *fully present*, which is something we could all learn from, and something animals can help bring into our lives, if we'll let them.

I knelt down in the grass in front of Winston, gently placed my hands on either side of his adorable black-and-white head, and looked him directly in the eyes. What I saw transfixed me. I saw intelligence. Personality. And an innocence so pure it could take your breath away. I bent forward, touched my forehead to his, and just stayed that way for a while, enjoying the moment. Emotion started to bubble up within me, and I felt tears in my eyes. Whatever troubles and anxieties I had brought into this beautiful pasture with me were released. There was no place for them here. I was touched, and the moment was highly cathartic. Winston was a frail baby who was fighting for his life, and yet he managed to give me some peace and healing. And he brought me into the present moment with him.

Sadly, Winston's weakened immune system was unable to fend off infection, and he would soon pass. Thankfully, he experienced a lot of love in his short life at the sanctuary, and in that time, he made a lasting impression on those fortunate enough to meet him, including me.

One of the greatest keys to happiness and leading a full life is to practice mindfulness—to quiet your thoughts and be fully present, without distraction. Being mindful allows you to achieve a heightened awareness of your environment and whatever you're experiencing, including those small moments that tend to go by unnoticed. There are miracles all around us in everyday life, and if you can learn to see the exquisite beauty in simple things and lean into it with intention, it can fill you with joy.

> "Too many people are dreaming of some magical rose garden on the horizon rather than enjoying the one growing in our backyards."
> —*Robin Sharma*

While mindfulness can elicit positive feelings, the benefits are substantially more far-reaching. There is a growing body of scientific research demonstrating that mindfulness, which has its roots in Buddhism, can contribute to improvements in many different areas of physical and mental health, including reducing anxiety and depression, lowering blood pressure, improving sleep, and even helping people manage pain. According to Dr. Zev Schuman-Olivier of Harvard University, "For many chronic illnesses, mindfulness meditation seems to improve quality of life and reduce mental health symptoms."[3] In addition to the medical benefits, there are a host of positive contributions to wellness whose value is significant yet difficult to quantify. Among other things, it has been shown to improve people's ability to connect with others and strengthen their capacity to deal with adversity. And studies have found that by pulling people out of the quagmire of their thoughts, mindfulness contributes to their feelings of happiness, sense of well-being, and overall satisfaction with life.

Unfortunately, despite its compelling benefits, practicing mindfulness is all too rare, primarily because it's more challenging than ever. To begin with, life is hard, and we get all wrapped up in ourselves. We have a lot to cope with. Our minds are perpetually on overdrive trying to process everything that has happened in the past, dwelling on things that either didn't go right or perhaps could have gone better. We carry our past around with us like a big sack full of heavy books that we keep adding to and re-reading. And then we're constantly projecting into the future, scanning the horizon—sometimes with longing, other times with trepidation. When we look to the future through a lens of fear, not only are we unable to appreciate the present moment, but we condemn ourselves to, in the words of Stoic philosopher Seneca, "suffer more in imagination than in reality," anticipating what might happen and torturing ourselves unnecessarily.

What do we tend to focus on the least? *The here and now*.

"As soon as you honor the present moment, unhappiness and struggle dissolve, and life begins to flow with joy and ease."
—*Eckhart Tolle*

We all manage to live in the present to some extent or another because it's necessary in order to survive, but *how* we live in the present makes all the difference. We're too often distracted and far from stillness. We've been born into a chaotic world where busyness is a badge of honor and everything competes for our attention. We are assailed by marketing and all manner of stimuli designed to lure us in: sights, sounds, and smells specifically engineered to entice our interest. And technology has escalated this phenomenon to unhealthy levels, causing epidemics of mental health disorders and disease. Social media and video platforms have become some of the most pervasive and absorbing distractions, meticulously crafted to pull us in with a force that is nothing short of pernicious. Our ability to process vast inputs, extract key pieces, and draw conclusions is a valuable skill—it allows us to navigate the world. To see things before they happen and make fewer mistakes. But as with most areas of life, problems arise when things get too far out of balance. Humans weren't designed to be inundated to the extremes normalized in modern day life. We weren't meant to be glued to phones or video screens. Or for our psyches to be incessantly flooded with sensationalized news, violent video games, or trash TV. Complicating the entire matter is that most of us are willing participants. Life is challenging, and distractions can be alluring. Lighting up our brains by indulging our senses offers an enticing escape from reality.

Another common distraction, and one I have fallen victim to at times, is work, which can be just as much of an avoidance behavior as binge-watching a reality TV show or indulging in a pint of your favorite ice cream. In moderation, such things are fine. But they are not good coping mechanisms and, when taken to extremes or used to avoid facing life, can be problematic. Not only do they consume time that could be spent practicing mindfulness, but they throw gasoline on the fire of our anxieties. It's hard to address underlying issues or be mindful when you're obsessed with clawing your way out of the black hole of work or comparing yourself to the selective snippets of perfection portrayed in social media feeds. Distractions can give us a feeling of control and have a tendency to become addictive. Over time our senses are dulled, prompting us to take things to greater extremes. Something that started sweet turns sickly. It's a nasty loop, and rarely ends well.

Given this backdrop, I have struggled to practice mindfulness. To keep my mind uncluttered and experience the amazing things in life that are all around me. It's still not easy, but I've made great efforts and strides because it's important. I don't want life to pass me by any more than it already has, and I want to be at peace. Mindfulness is one of the greatest gifts we can give ourselves, and it's something we're all capable of. We just need to realize our innate capacity. To unlock our potential. What is the key to unlocking this ability? While I don't think there is a single answer to this question, there are three steps that I have found beneficial. It starts with laying the groundwork: acknowledging the powerful impediments to mindfulness within ourselves and modern society, and marshaling the will to tame them.

> "Be where you are, otherwise you will miss your life."
> —*Buddha*

1 – Setting Yourself up for Success

While I've had a basic familiarity with the concept of mindfulness for many years, I was slow to embrace it as a practice, and efforts I made were met with a lot of resistance. Arguably, the biggest single step I made toward being mindful was to develop a higher level of awareness, both within myself and with regards to the world around me. Observing the voice in my head that was incessantly dwelling on the past or worrying about the future and recognizing the amount of stress that such thoughts were causing. I had to notice all the things around me that were competing for my attention and acknowledge the degree to which I was allowing it to happen. You have to see things as they truly are before you can take steps to change them.

The other prerequisite to change is having the motivation to take the necessary steps and the discipline to sustain them. As someone whose mind relentlessly races, I found being present without distraction uncomfortable. Practices designed to foster presence, such as meditation, felt foreign and difficult. Stepping away from the distractions I had grown accustomed to, or even curbing them, was unsettling. When you're used to mainlining stimulation and traveling at high speeds, it's challenging to unplug and bring things to a crawl, even for short periods of time. In these situations, I found myself gravitating toward any excuse or readily available distraction, so I have learned to establish boundaries. To do things like turning off my phone, not checking social media, or setting aside a block of uninterrupted time that is specifically dedicated to a healthy activity that lends itself well to being present, like meditation or a walk. I've also found it helpful to set daily goals, a habit that can be assisted through apps or journaling. Just making the commitment to being deliberately present one time each day is a great place to start. It will help you get more comfortable with the concept, and over time you'll experience the benefits. If you find yourself forgetting or needing additional motivation, block the time out in your calendar and set reminders, or maybe find an accountability partner—someone close to you who you can share your commitment with. Over time practicing mindfulness will become more routine, and you can try to incorporate additional moments of mindfulness throughout your day.

"Mindfulness isn't difficult. We just need to remember to do it."
—*Sharon Salzberg*

2 – Being Present

The actual practice of mindfulness doesn't need to be any more complicated than you choose to make it: it simply involves following through on an intention to be aware and present without judgment or distraction. That said, there are a lot of techniques that people use to foster mindfulness and practice it more effectively, and I encourage you to explore them. There are numerous books, apps, and online resources readily available. Regardless of what approach you may take, it starts with a high level of intentionality—making a conscious decision to be fully aware and present in a given moment. From this point, people employ a variety of tactics, including meditation and breathing exercises, which are popular and effective practices to help facilitate mindfulness by stilling the mind and improving focus. But while breath work and other meditative practices cultivate mindfulness, they are not prerequisites. Personally, while I meditate and find it beneficial, I elect to take a different approach when practicing mindfulness. For example, while my experience with meditation in the Buddhist temple (Chapter 10) instilled a sense of transcendence and connectedness, the path was deeply inward, whereas with mindfulness, my senses are heightened and I'm focused on being closely attuned with my environment. That said, some of the methods I use to help facilitate mindfulness include meditative aspects.

To help settle my mind, I will often start by taking a few long, slow, deep breaths, in through my nose and out through my mouth. This is a well-established relaxation technique that triggers a host of beneficial physiological responses, calming the sympathetic nervous system and reducing feelings of stress. In addition to quieting my mind in order to be more present, I will also use this technique when I feel rising levels of anxiety.

I will observe my thoughts without judgment, and take a step back from them, consciously clearing my mind and shifting my focus to the current moment. When I notice my mind wandering, I gently return my attention to the present and what's around me.

I carefully observe my surroundings, paying close attention to all five senses and what I'm experiencing. Since I have a tendency to rely heavily on my sight, it's sometimes helpful to close my eyes initially and heighten focus on sound, smell, taste, and touch. And when my eyes are open, I try to intensify my observance and examine things more closely than usual. To see the veins on a leaf, the colors in a painting, or the intricate patterns of a spider web—the things I wouldn't typically notice. Only then will I open up and take in the totality of my surroundings.

> "Life is a curtain that hides the divine. You can peek behind that when you quiet the mind."
> —*Mike Posner*

While it can be helpful to deliberately and deeply engage in practicing mindfulness using techniques such as these, the ultimate goal is to learn to incorporate mindfulness throughout the day, noticing small beautiful things and experiencing a sense of wonder without needing to approach mindfulness in a structured way. Or, when engaged with another person, giving your full attention, free of distractions, and being present with them completely.

3 – Seeing the Miracles All around You

One of the most striking things about the specific moments of mindfulness I share in the opening stories of this chapter is how ordinary they were on the surface. Most people have periodic interactions with animals in some fashion or another, and even urban centers have parks where we can get a restorative dose of nature. The natural world is where humans evolved, and it has a unique power to facilitate an undistracted, healthy presence. That said, it's possible to practice mindfulness in any location and under any circumstance. Buddhist monk Thích Nhất Hạnh, known as the "father of mindfulness," famously uses dishwashing as an example. "If while washing dishes, we think only of the cup of tea that awaits us, thus hurrying to get the dishes out of the way as if they were a nuisance, then we are not 'washing the dishes to wash the dishes.' What's more, we are not alive during the time we are washing the dishes. In fact, we are completely incapable of realizing the miracle of life while standing at the sink."[4]

As with Thích Nhất Hạnh's eloquent example, the episodes I recounted earlier don't stand out as much because of the natural environment or the rarity of the situation as because of the degree to which I was present and undistracted, which allowed me to connect and experience something at a higher level. This can be true for everything in life—it can either be perceived as mundane or offer something deeper. As Ralph Waldo Emerson wrote, "The invariable mark of wisdom is to see the miraculous in the common." Hopefully I will someday be wise enough to sustain mindfulness, even while doing menial tasks such as washing the dishes, because the implications are profound. You don't need to chase extraordinary experiences to be happy. The world around us provides endless opportunities to feel joy.

> "Everything has its beauty, but not everyone sees it."
> —Andy Warhol

In his delightful book *Small Graces: The Quiet Gifts of Everyday Life*, author Kent Nerburn recounts a time when he posed a hypothetical question to a blind friend: if she were to have the opportunity to regain her sight long enough to see just one thing in the entire world, what would it be? Expecting her to respond with something grand or exotic, he is taken aback at her answer: clouds. She could imagine almost everything that people described to her in detail, but not clouds. They sounded so extraordinary, but she just couldn't picture them in her mind. When I first read Nerburn's story, I found it deeply impactful, primarily because it reminded me both how much I take for granted and how little I pay attention to the beauty and miracles all around me every day. As a child, I would lie on my back and look at clouds with wonder and imagination, but how long had it been since I'd marveled at them with the innocence of youth? How many other things was I missing? And how blessed was I to be alive and have the opportunity to experience such things?

WHAT DO I WANT FOR YOU?

I want you to recognize and appreciate the power of being present without distraction. To know the happiness and peace that mindfulness can bring into your life.

I want you to be aware of all the internal and external forces distracting you and causing you to dwell on the past or the future—the voices in your head, the pushes and pulls of daily living, and the myriad of technologies and efforts fighting for your attention. To acknowledge how challenging it can be to practice mindfulness, but to also understand the rewards and know it's worth the effort.

I want you to have the resolve to establish boundaries and put yourself in a position to be mindful. To overcome the discomfort associated with stillness. To explore the methods and practices designed to aid you in being present, and to embrace those that work for you. To cultivate an ability to see and savor the things that most people miss. To find beauty and sacredness in the ordinary.

I want you to learn how to slow down, heighten your senses, and fully experience life. To view the world around you with reverence, wonder, and curiosity, and to feel the unbridled joy and tranquility it can bring. To regularly stop and give the people and world around you your undivided attention. To bear witness to the miracles that are all around you.

I want you to, in the words of Mother Teresa, "be happy in the moment. That is enough."

15

POSITIVITY

A Cornerstone of Happiness

>Keep your face always toward the sunshine—
>and shadows will fall behind you.
>—*Walt Whitman*

>Perpetual optimism is a force multiplier.
>—*Colin Powell*

"We're overworked, and I'm sick of it," said a professor a few rows down from me. Other faculty members voiced their agreement and added their own complaints, which were wide-ranging, and the negativity spread like wildfire. Each cynical comment emboldened others to speak up and spew their own vitriol. I was thirty-seven years old and had been teaching at the local college for less than a year. This was the first time I had attended one of the monthly union meetings, and I was completely taken aback by the bitterness and entitlement. Personally, I was excited to be teaching and grateful for the light work schedule. Per the terms of the union contract, faculty members only had to teach 156 days per year, and that limit was strictly adhered to. We had a flexible schedule, got the entire summer off, plus a boatload of extended breaks and holidays. Being a college professor was certainly not without its challenges, but having recently left the corporate world, the assertion that we were overworked seemed preposterous. Believing my fellow faculty could benefit from my perspective, I felt compelled to speak up. Unsurprisingly, my notions were not well received.

Through my previous work experience, I had seen firsthand how damaging negativity can be. It's like a fast-spreading disease, and I didn't want anything to do with it. Staying positive was a priority for me, and a critical part of that was being careful about who I spent time with. In this respect, the union meeting was toxic, and when I spoke up, I felt alone. But afterward, I was pleasantly surprised to be approached by several faculty members who thanked me. They shared my view and appreciated my words. While I would teach at the college for nearly a decade, I never attended another union meeting. Instead, I would make concerted efforts to associate with colleagues who shared my gratitude and positive mindset. I would also tap into a wellspring of positive energy by focusing on my teaching and serving my students to the best of my ability.

"I don't know what to do," my advisee said in a tormented voice. "Whatever I decide to major in is going to determine what I do for the rest of my life." She paused for a moment, fidgeting and fearful. "What if I get it *wrong?*" she asked with rising alarm. "My future would be *ruined.*" She was being so dramatic that it might have been comical if she wasn't in such obvious distress.

Part of my job as a professor involved student advising, which I enjoyed. This particular advisee was feeling overwhelmed by decisions surrounding what to study. "It's completely okay to not know what you want to do," I told her. "I'm in my forties, and I'm still trying to figure out what I want to be when I grow up."

There was a look of puzzlement on her face as she tried to process what I had just said. "What do you mean?" she asked.

"Well, I studied engineering in college. But after doing that for five years, I realized it wasn't for me. So I quit and joined the Peace Corps. And then I decided to attend business school. After that I worked as a management consultant, and then I went to work at an internet startup. That wasn't a good fit, so now I'm teaching. And I recently started a real estate business. Who knows what I'll do next. I keep trying things, and if they don't work, then I just do something else."

"But doesn't it bother you that you wasted all that time studying things you don't do anymore?" she asked. "And every time you change careers you have to start all over again."

"That's one way to look at it," I responded. "But I just don't think it's reasonable to expect anyone to have their entire life all figured out at your age. In my case, I'm still not sure. Once I accepted that life isn't a one-act play and it's okay to change directions, I had the freedom to do what feels right. But in my opinion, nothing I've done has been a waste of time. It all shaped me in various ways. It honed transferable skills and broadened my perspective. I met interesting people and enjoyed rewarding experiences. I also learned a lot about myself."

She was nodding, and I could tell my message was getting through. "But if you kept changing, then you must not have been happy," she said.

"There are always aspects of jobs and life that are unpleasant, and that's okay. We also make mistakes and have setbacks. We can't always control these things, but we can choose how we respond to them. You can dwell on your circumstances, feeling stuck and sorry for yourself, in which case you'll likely be consumed with negativity. Or you can approach your situation with a higher level of awareness, acceptance, and even gratitude. You can learn from the negative things you experience and derive motivation to make changes for the better. When you don't like something, that's valuable information—you're learning about yourself, and it's like a clue or waypoint on your journey showing you where to go."

My advisee had a contemplative look on her face as she tried to process everything I had just said. I realized it was time to bring the conversation back around to her current situation.

POSITIVITY

"So, to answer your question, of course I haven't always been happy with everything, but I do the best I can to look for the positive in the negative. Because nothing good is going to happen if you don't have a positive mindset. Positivity can help you find peace where you're at and allow you to grow out of it and make different choices. I would encourage you to just make the best decision you can right now regarding your studies, but to know that no matter what you choose to do, it's the right decision. You'll either be happy with it, or you'll learn valuable lessons and use that to guide and motivate you to chart a new course. Nobody expects you to know right now what you want to do for the rest of your life. And it's okay."

She smiled, and I knew that my words had made an impact. "Thank you," she said, with obvious relief. I could see the depth of her gratitude, and in that moment, I counted my own blessings. It was fulfilling to help others, and I would always be a teacher at heart.

While it can sometimes be a struggle for me to maintain a positive mindset, I am very aware of how important it is to see the good and hopeful aspects of life. Positivity is a cornerstone of happiness, and my experience in business and life has made it apparent that outcomes are closely correlated with the quality of my thoughts. It doesn't matter if I'm running a race, trying to land a real estate deal, or coping with a health issue. Positivity has an uncanny way of manifesting itself. In that way, positivity is like generosity—the nature of the energy you embody and put out into the world comes back to you. There was a time in my life when I would have scoffed at such a notion, but the benefits of cultivating a positive mindset have been well documented, perhaps most notably by author Napoleon Hill.

> "Your attitude, how you look at the world,
> will determine what you get in life."
> —*Robert Greene*

According to Hill, the trajectory of his life was forever altered in 1908 when he met Andrew Carnegie, one of the most successful business tycoons of his era. Carnegie suggested that Hill study the most accomplished people in the world to determine the underlying keys to their success. Hill accepted the challenge, and purportedly spent the next two decades of his life analyzing major historical figures and interviewing more than five hundred luminaries of the time, including entrepreneurs like Henry Ford, Thomas Edison, and John D. Rockefeller, and even presidents Theodore Roosevelt and Howard Taft. Hill would eventually summarize his findings in the classic *Think and Grow Rich*, which became one of the bestselling self-help books of all time.

In *Think and Grow Rich*, Hill presents a host of principles proven to yield success. But his core premise is that a life of abundance can be achieved by harnessing the incredible power of the mind. He calls on the reader to exercise the utmost care in cultivating their thoughts and attitudes. To cast aside negativity and instead foster a deep faith, definiteness of purpose, and positive outlook. Hill determined that the energy of our thoughts manifests in the physical world. Think negative, and it will be self-fulfilling. Think positive and believe strongly enough, and the forces of the universe will align to help you achieve your dreams.

In addition to helping dreams come to fruition, maintaining a positive state of mind has been shown to significantly improve wellness. According to the Mayo Clinic, positivity and optimism (an inclination to expect favorable outcomes) have been shown to increase happiness and improve our ability to manage stress while providing a host of positive health benefits that can increase life span, including reduced risk of cardiovascular disease, respiratory conditions, and even cancer.[5] Positive people also tend to have healthier relationships and lifestyle habits, which improves overall mental and physical well-being.

Negativity, on the other hand, has been shown to undermine wellness by raising stress levels and making people more susceptible to health problems, low self-esteem, depression, and anxiety. Negativity can take many different forms, and goes well beyond seeing the glass of water as half empty. Examples include taking things personally, blaming, assuming or predicting the worst (pessimism), overblowing problems, judging yourself or others, or fixating on the negative aspects of a situation while minimizing the positive ones. It can surface outwardly through behaviors such as complaining, provocative comments, and criticism, or in less direct behaviors such as gossip, sarcasm, or passive aggressiveness.

How do you curtail such thinking and behaviors? It's not easy, particularly when negative attitudes have become deeply ingrained over time. But like any other bad habit, it can be changed. Both positivity and negativity are primarily rooted in self-talk, which is the conversation going on in your head. This inner monologue is the result of many different factors, both internal and external, and changing self-talk for the better is both within our control and the key to adopting a more optimistic viewpoint.

> "Choose to be optimistic, it feels better."
> —*The Fourteenth Dalai Lama*

External factors are important because maintaining positivity in the face of overwhelmingly negative influences can feel like trying to walk up a down escalator—it's difficult to maintain forward momentum, it's draining, and it's not likely to end well. Negativity is also highly contagious, and the more of it we're exposed to, the more difficult it is to sustain a positive outlook. You can think of your environment and what you consume as seeds, and these seeds get planted in the fertile garden of your mind. It's how thoughts propagate. The first step in maintaining a positive attitude is to ensure you're planting flowers and not weeds. To take heed of what you're exposed to and reduce the negative influences.

First and foremost, limiting your exposure to negativity starts with who you're listening to and spending time with. Whenever possible, try to surround yourself with positive people and information, both in real life and virtually. In my own life, I avoid negative people as much as possible, and I've carefully curated my social media feeds by unfollowing people or hiding content that is divisive, fear-based, or hostile. I spend far less time on social media than I used to, but when I do log in, I am able to consume content that is almost exclusively motivational, educational, and uplifting. I also consume positive books, podcasts, and videos. In these and other ways, I plant and tend to seeds that will grow to my benefit, fostering peace of mind and positivity.

"Folks are usually about as happy as they make up their minds to be."
—*Abraham Lincoln*

It's a good idea to periodically take inventory of the physical and virtual company you're keeping and set boundaries. On multiple occasions I've seen one negative person disrupt an entire high-functioning team. It's like when you take a piece of bright-colored laundry and mix it with a load of whites—everything ends up tainted. If you can't keep your distance physically, do it mentally. Just because someone is talking doesn't mean you need to listen or care what they think. And you certainly shouldn't agree or vocalize anything that reinforces what you're hearing, which is a surefire way for the seeds of negativity to take root within you. Instead of engaging, exercise detachment and let things pass through you. Author Mel Robbins suggests building a "positivity shield" to protect yourself from all the negative energy that comes at you throughout the day—creating a kind of energetic forcefield whereby you can protect yourself from the inside out. It may also help to internally repeat a mantra or positive affirmation. Mentally disconnecting from toxic influences in this manner can help maintain equanimity and preserve a positive mindset.

While attending to external factors is certainly helpful, there is greater progress to be made with internal work. Our own thoughts and words are so much more powerful than most of us give them credit for, and exercising control is fundamental to maintaining a positive outlook. As former monk and author Jay Shetty says, "Change begins with the words inside your head." Shifting our inner monologue is not easy, but it's certainly possible. And it's definitely worthwhile. What follows are four strategies that I have found to be effective, starting with how to view adversity.

1 – Reframe Adversity

There are not a lot of certainties in life, but here's one—we will all face hardship and setbacks. Because we are human, we'll make mistakes. We will fail. We will experience loss, hurt, and pain. And while the extent of such trials may vary, they will be experienced to some degree on a daily basis. Adversity is a necessary and valuable part of life. Unfortunately, most people don't view it that way—particularly when they experience something deeply hurtful. But we all know people who are perpetually disappointed when even small things don't go perfectly—which they almost never do. And the feelings that such an unrealistic mindset engenders aren't healthy ones. They may feel singled out, persecuted, unlucky, or unworthy. How many of us, faced with adversity, have said "why me?" or "just my luck!" Such responses are defeatist and can foster a sense of hopelessness or victimhood. They breathe life into whatever difficulty is being faced, and sometimes perpetuate it, putting bad energy out into the world. Instead of reacting to adversity with negativity, ask yourself what the universe is trying to tell you. Use it as an opportunity to learn and grow.

When we face adversity it's also an opportunity to test ourselves and evolve. Stoic philosopher Seneca said, "No man is more unhappy than he who never faces adversity. For he is not permitted to prove himself." Seneca said this because adversity is a necessary part of progress, and it makes us better humans. It reveals character and builds resilience. Viewing hardship from a position of deep negativity is like hating a piece of exercise equipment. A rowing machine, weights, or a bicycle are not inherently bad things. They provide the resistance that can make us stronger and healthier. If we avoided all physical challenges, we would be weak and vulnerable. The same principles apply to facing adversity. You can cultivate positivity by embracing this truth and recognizing the inherent value in things like setbacks and mistakes. By knowing they are surmountable and will pass. By being resilient, overcoming, and moving forward. Onward and upward, we grow. Hardships can also be viewed as a counterbalance necessary to experience the joys in life—the downs help us to fully savor and appreciate the ups. In the words of Martin Luther King Jr., "Only in the darkness can you see the stars." For better or worse, we all experience adversity, and we're better off accepting it as an important and valuable part of life.

> "We cannot create happiness in a place where there is no suffering, just as we cannot grow lotuses without mud."
> —*Thích Nhất Hạnh*

My views on hardship were influenced by my running coach Ian Sharman, who taught me to consider all the things that could go wrong in an ultramarathon and envision how I will react and overcome them. Because things rarely go as planned. Being aware of this and accepting it ahead of time made me less likely to be derailed when things went awry. It trained me to accept setbacks as part of the overall experience. It mentally prepared me to manage situations as they arose and allowed me to feel a greater sense of appreciation and accomplishment when I persevered. When in the midst of facing adversity, it's also difficult to remain objective, so Ian advised me to give myself the advice I'd give a friend under the same circumstances, which I have found to be a great piece of wisdom. These lessons I learned from Ian have proven even more valuable when applied in other areas of life. The power that setbacks have to cause negativity can be mitigated by awareness, acceptance, perseverance, and self-compassion, which we will cover later in this chapter.

> "Where would the gardener be if there were no more weeds?"
> —Chuang-Tzu

Author Byron Katie also encourages reframing our views on negativity. "Life is simple," she says. "Everything happens for you, not to you. Everything happens at exactly the right moment, neither too soon nor too late. You don't have to like it . . . It's just easier if you do." While it may not be easy, adopting the perspective that life happens *for* you can be a potent mental framework. To look at it any other way, says Katie, is to oppose reality, which causes suffering. There is peace of mind in knowing that things are the way they were meant to be. That everything happens for a reason and is ultimately for the better. In psychological circles, changing your subjective interpretation of your circumstances in this manner is called cognitive reappraisal, and it can be a highly effective tool for maintaining positivity.

2 – Avoid the 4 C's

Our thoughts and words heavily influence our perception of the world, and the narratives we repeat to ourselves affect how we live our lives. While the voices in our monkey minds can take many different forms and run away in a thousand directions, there are some thought patterns and habits that are particularly pernicious, and those include comparing, complaining, criticizing, and catastrophizing. Each of these four C's can take root and snowball in ways that fuel negativity.

The first C is Comparison. Comparing yourself with others is a natural inclination, but it can also be harmful. There's a reason people call comparison "the thief of joy." It tends to make us envious of others and ungrateful for what we already have, which causes stress and makes it difficult to be happy. And the problem is exacerbated by an endless world of people we might elect to stack ourselves up against—we can find ourselves trapped in an endless loop, where nothing is enough. Other people are also a terrible metric because everyone is different and we rarely have enough knowledge to get an accurate gauge of someone else's full circumstances. That's why social media is a virtual comparison cesspool—most people online frame themselves in the best possible light, which distorts our perspective and makes us feel less than. Instead of comparing, try to focus on noticing the good things in your own life. Embrace the one thing you're the best at in the entire world—*being yourself*. In the words of Dr. Seuss, "There is no one alive who is you-er than you!" And if you're going to compare at all, consider examining the versions of yourself that have evolved over time. Strive to be a more self-actualized person today than you were yesterday.

The second and third C's are Criticizing and Complaining, which are habit-forming ways of verbalizing negative emotions and discontent. These behaviors perpetuate negative thought patterns and make bad feelings worse, which can be detrimental to our physical and emotional well-being. They also put bad energy out into the world and can be toxic to those around us—particularly if directed at another person. That said, things don't always go right, and open communication will sometimes require you to point out things that bother you. While there is nothing inherently wrong with expressing our feelings, don't allow your negative statements to become chronic, and try to be as kind, objective, and impersonal as possible in how you deliver the message. Regulating behavior in this manner isn't easy, but the rewards are plentiful. A great exercise is to commit to not complaining or criticizing for a specific time period, such as an hour, the length of a shift at work, or even for an entire day (much harder than it sounds). You can also try not using specific words like "should," or adding a "but" to the end of any complaint to highlight something good. Gamifying it in these ways helps build awareness and interrupts destructive thoughts.

> "Words can shape the way we think and feel, which is then reflected in our outcomes. Meaning that if we continually use certain words or phrases, they will become self-fulfilling."
> —*Tony Robbins*

The last C is Catastrophizing, which is a tendency to inflate situations beyond reason and fixate on the worst possible outcome. This cognitive distortion tends to emerge during times of stress, and it's dangerous because it can take people on a deep and rapid downward spiral, often in response to something completely unrealistic or outside their control. Catastrophizing is often associated with a propensity to look at things linearly and not on a spectrum—all good or all bad. This is called "dichotomous thinking," and it's dangerous because it's so limiting. Looking at things in such a black-and-white manner doesn't allow for middle ground and can lead to bad conclusions, catastrophic or otherwise. Such habits are often rooted in anxiety or low self-esteem and can be difficult to break. It's not easy to change the story in our heads, especially when the catastrophe in question can be rationalized through selective data or the media, which often perpetuates and reinforces our fears, making it difficult to keep things in proper perspective.

Moving past a tendency to make problems bigger than they are requires awareness and interruption of our irrational thoughts. Focus on changing self-talk and replacing the negative outcome with a positive one. Be optimistic but also realistic. It's okay to believe that bad things happen sometimes, as long as you don't dwell or go to extremes. Bad times are a normal part of life, and their occurrence doesn't mean that everything will go terribly wrong. The sky is not going to fall, and things are almost always better than they seem. Life has a wonderful way of working out, and there is strength in knowing that things are going to be okay again. That this too shall pass. In fact, while it may be difficult to accept in the moment, most things we're overly anxious about today, we won't even remember in a few years.

3 – Exercise Self-Compassion

The third strategy that has helped me to maintain a more positive mindset is self-compassion, which we touched on in Chapter 7. When it comes to self-talk, we all have a tendency to be our own worst critics. In fact, we're almost all harder on ourselves than we are on anyone else, and we often hold ourselves to impossibly high standards. The result? We fall short, which makes us feel like failures. It erodes our self-esteem and makes us unhappy. It's hard to maintain positivity when we judge and berate ourselves in this manner. Far better to be our own best allies. To nurture an internal wellspring of acceptance, kindness, and love for ourselves. This is where self-compassion comes in.

> "If we treated ourselves the way we treated our best friend, can you imagine how much better off we would be?"
> —*Meghan Markle*

Dr. Kristin Neff defines self-compassion as "the process of turning compassion inward. We are kind and understanding rather than harshly self-critical when we fail, make mistakes, or feel inadequate. We give ourselves support and encouragement rather than being cold and judgmental when challenges and difficulty arise in our lives." Dr. Neff is a professor at the University of Texas at Austin and a pioneer in the field of self-compassion. In her books and online course (which I completed), Dr. Neff encourages people to exercise self-kindness instead of self-judgment. To accept the reality of life and our humanity—that we're not perfect and things won't always go as planned. And to treat ourselves the same way we would treat a loved one—using the same language for our self-talk. Dr. Neff also stresses the need for a balanced approach to managing our emotions, with a focus on mindfulness versus overidentification. The goal is to be aware, nonjudgmental, and open, observing thoughts and feelings without letting our emotions run away with themselves or being consumed by negativity.

4 – Take Action

In *Think and Grow Rich*, Napoleon Hill says that "you have absolute control over but one thing, and this is your thoughts," an assertion that supports the first three strategies shared here. But when you're really struggling and marinating in negativity, changing self-talk can sometimes feel impossible. We can all get caught up in dark ruminations that are difficult to cope with. In times like these, it's easy to lose objectivity, and trying to restore a positive mindset can be particularly challenging. Willpower alone just isn't enough. How do you move forward? It's easier to control our behaviors than it is our thoughts and feelings, so instead of futilely wrestling with your irrational thoughts, take action as a way to regain positivity. Move your body or engage your mind. Physically do something that makes you feel good. My go-to is a walk or run, preferably in nature. Studies have shown that walks can improve your mood, especially in places where there is greenery.[6] But there are plenty of other options. Take a bath. Play with your pet. Call a loved one. Read a good book or listen to uplifting music. Bake something. Clean or organize something. Anything healthy that sparks joy for you. Doing an act of kindness or service for someone else is also a great antidote to negativity. Making yourself *do* any of these things can initiate a physiological response, reducing your stress, grounding your mind, and improving your outlook.

> "I try to engage in practices that lead to or cultivate more optimism, positivity, and gratitude in my life. And they all trace back to this idea of 'mood follows action' . . . If you want to shift your mental or emotional disposition, you have to do something to accomplish that."
> —*Rich Roll*

Finally, in addition to the four strategies outlined herein, I think it's important to note that in many ways, positivity is a byproduct of all the other lessons and principles shared throughout this book. Embracing gratitude, for example, is one of the most powerful ways to sustain a positive mindset. Practicing generosity, empathy, and spirituality can also foster positivity. So will being mindful, doing things that are uncomfortable, and attending to your overall wellness. These and other virtues and lessons covered in this book are interrelated—threads of the same tapestry that overlay one another, forming an intricate pattern that contributes to the whole.

WHAT DO I WANT FOR YOU?

I want you to recognize the importance of cultivating a positive mindset. To recognize the power of your thoughts—how they ultimately manifest themselves in the physical world and affect your quality of life.

I want you to take the necessary steps to manage the internal and external factors that influence your state of mind. To limit your exposure to negativity and be conscious of the seeds you are planting.

I want you to appreciate the power of your inner world and the importance of self-talk. To reframe hardship. To be resilient and see the silver lining. To avoid bad habits like comparing, complaining, and catastrophizing. To exercise self-compassion and take actions that will help you reinforce a positive outlook.

I want you to know that striving to sustain positivity is challenging, but it's worth the effort. I want you to feel the joy and contentment that positivity can bring, both into your own life and into the lives of others.

16

CONCLUSION

Closing Thoughts and Wishes

> Your whole life is one giant gift waiting for you to unwrap it.
> —*Mel Robbins*

> Do anything, but let it produce joy.
> —*Walt Whitman*

As I hiked up the trail's steep incline, a persistent voice in my head was peppering me with cynical questions, dredging up feelings of inadequacy, and stoking embers of self-doubt. I was feeling down and unmotivated, which seemed ironic given that I'd just written a chapter about positivity. "Who am I to be writing a book on life lessons?" I asked myself. "I can't even get my own sh*t together."

It was a hot summer morning in 2023, and my mind was awhirl with negative thoughts. It had been a challenging day right from the start. After waking up, I had lain in bed for hours, feeling depressed and struggling to find the motivation to start the day. It didn't matter that, in my estimation, the dour mood was unjustified. Yes, I had problems in my life, and some were significant. But so did everyone else. And I had so much to be grateful for. I knew this. Yet on that day even the smallest difficulties loomed irrationally large, and in aggregate they produced a weight that felt difficult to bear. Eventually, I managed to crawl out of bed and muddle through some of my morning routines, but nothing I tried seemed to make a difference.

In fact, things were getting worse, and I knew I had to do something. My inner critic was on overdrive and gaining momentum. Remembering that mood follows action, I decided to head to a nearby trail for a run. I was aware of what was going on inside myself, and I knew this was my best chance to turn things around. After arriving at the trailhead, I sat in my Jeep procrastinating and felt a strong urge to return home. The resistance was real. "But I already changed my clothes and drove here," I told myself. I looked down at the trail running shoes on my feet for confirmation. "I at least have to go for a damn walk," I said out loud. And off I went, my head still swirling with caustic thoughts. Though my struggles were mental, I felt physically drained. And this is how I found myself hiking up the hill, plagued with doubts and questioning myself about my writing and my worthiness.

But after about twenty minutes of walking, something magical started to happen. The haze began to slowly lift, and the burden gradually lessened. My trudge turned into a slow jog, and eventually a run. Being in nature and moving my body was gradually evaporating my negativity, like the sun burning off a morning fog. And as that fog dispersed, my positive self-talk and gratitude finally began to gain some purchase. I breathed deeply, inhaling the fresh mountain air. For the first time, I noticed the beauty all around me, which brought me further relief. My pace quickened as I felt a bit lighter. I reminded myself of the blessings in my life, including you. There were stirrings of peace and joy. I mustered up some much-needed self-compassion. "I'm not perfect, but I've come a long way," I told myself. "I got myself out here today and turned things around. Everything is going to be okay. I'm doing the best I can. And that's enough."

CONCLUSION

> "Happiness is not something ready-made.
> It comes from your own actions."
> —*The Fourteenth Dalai Lama*

Reading the stories, reflections, and lessons in this book, you might draw the conclusion that I've now mastered life in some fashion. That I've cultivated the perfect garden. But that would be a terribly inaccurate conclusion. Yes, I've learned a lot, but I don't have it all figured out. Nobody does. I definitely struggle, just like everyone else. Life can be hard at times. Things happen that test my limits. And there are also days that are difficult for no apparent reason, when happiness seems beyond my reach. I know this is normal—nobody is happy all the time, but that doesn't make it any less real. So I do my best. I employ the tools in my toolkit like meditation, gratitude, and movement. I foster resilience and practice the things that help me lead my best life. And while my efforts do make a difference, I remain far from perfect. In fact, at this stage in my journey, the two things I am perhaps most sure about are how flawed I am and how little I actually know. But thankfully, I'm at peace with these facts. I'm human, and life is a wonderful teacher, so I know I'll never stop learning. I'll never stop growing. I'll be tending my garden for the rest of my days. The journey of self-actualization never ends, and that's okay. It's a journey I'm grateful and privileged to be on. I'm excited to see where it takes me.

> "The only true wisdom is in knowing you know nothing."
> —*Socrates*

It is my hope that you can approach life with a similar mindset. That you can be humble, self-aware, and grateful. Know how much you don't know. Commit to growth but recognize and accept your own limitations and imperfections. Because none of us are perfect. Welcome to the human experience. Instead, we are *perfectly imperfect*.

CONCLUSION

Better to accept your fallibility early in life and save yourself a lot of angst. Be as compassionate with yourself as you are with loved ones. Silence the inner critic (Chapter 15). Laugh at yourself. Know you are enough, and love yourself (Chapter 7). Take some of that self-imposed pressure off and find a little peace.

I realize that such things are far easier said than done. And I can relate to how difficult it can sometimes be to move in the right direction, even when the path is clear. Just because I've gained some wisdom or recognized a truth doesn't mean I've perfected it, or even fully embraced it. Knowing a principle or practice on an intellectual level is very different from internalizing it and living it. And things are rarely as straightforward as they initially seem. Life is full of subtleties, paradoxes, and contradictions, some of which have surfaced in this book. But the knowledge we assimilate provides a roadmap for growth, and hopefully you'll learn some things and derive value from what I've shared.

I've been a prolific reader for a long time, and I know there are limits to how transformative a book can be. How much it can really sink in and make a difference. When I read a good book, a light bulb will sometimes go on. It can make a mark. And then it becomes a small part of me—something I carry forward. But there is no substitute for living through something and experiencing it firsthand. Life can teach and crystalize lessons in a way that writing will never be able to match. And the notions and opinions of any individual author, including myself, should be viewed through a lens of skepticism. Of course it's okay to consider the advice and opinions of authors, mentors, loved ones, and others, as long as you don't weigh them too heavily. Don't ever outsource your thinking and decision-making. Be curious, and give what others say due consideration, but don't be easily swayed. In fact, the more persuasive and emphatic a person is, the more wary and skeptical you should be. Question everything. Stay vigilant but open, and *seek truth*. Value diverse perspectives and resist gravitating to people and content that serve only to reinforce and rationalize your thoughts and opinions—this kind of "confirmation bias" may feel

CONCLUSION

good but ultimately fosters ignorance. Absorb as much knowledge as you can, but be discerning and make up your own mind about things. Adopt a default of curiosity, kindness, and wonder. And when it makes sense to do so, change your position.

> "Trust thyself: every heart vibrates to that iron string."
> —*Ralph Waldo Emerson*

Who can provide you with the best advice? Yourself. As Mel Robbins says in her book *The 5 Second Rule*, "Your inner wisdom is a genius." Listen to your heart, and always do what feels right. The best path for you to walk is the one that is uniquely yours. It's definitely not my path—I want better for you. And it's not anyone else's path. Make the life you want for yourself, whatever that is. Do what will bring you joy and peace of mind because that's worth more than gold. One of my many takeaways from my trip to Everest Base Camp came from observing and interacting with the Nepali people, who made a deeper impression than the Himalayas. I encountered people who were truly kind, generous, and happy. They were present and joyful, despite living in conditions of hardship, with limited material possessions or resources. They led simple, spiritual lives with hearts full of joy, compassion, and gratitude. I observed the same thing during my Peace Corps service in the Dominican Republic. Many of the people I befriended embodied a happiness that comes from having few wants, serving others, and leading a life of abundance in the areas that truly matter. This is real wealth. A wealth that can't be realized through materialistic conquests and superficial attainments. Being relaxed and happy in life is more valuable than a prestigious job or a fat bank account.

While I encourage you to have a growth mindset, it doesn't have to be career-oriented. Remember that the most meaningful pursuits are often more personal or spiritual in nature (Chapter 10). This is why a critical part of growth is taking time to unwind and be present. Don't let life pass you by. Learn from the past, plan for the future, but don't lose sight of what's right in front of you. When you work or create, fall in love with the process and savor it (Chapters 4 and 5). Find joy in the simple things (Chapter 14). But you don't always have to be doing things. Allow yourself time to just *be*. As Buddhist monk Thích Nhất Hạnh said, "We think that when we are not doing anything, we are wasting our time. But that is not true. Our time is first of all for us to be. To be what? To be alive, to be peaceful, to be joyful, to be loving. And that is what the world needs most."

Whatever you're seeking, be it material or spiritual, don't expect it to fall in your lap. Wherever you decide to go in life, be prepared to make it happen. Take ownership of yourself and your destiny (Chapter 2). Chart your own course, and be proactive and deliberate in your choices and your actions. Don't be deterred by doubt and fears—you're capable of far more than you realize (Chapter 3). Foster a sense of agency, and make your own luck. Abraham Lincoln said, "The best way to predict the future is to create it." Don't follow the path life places before you—forge your own. And accept that things will not go smoothly. Life is a series of setbacks, and how it unfolds will in large part depend on how you choose to view and react to all the obstacles placed in your path. We can elect to see hardships as welcome opportunities for learning and growth (Chapters 6 and 15). Or we can feel victimized and stew in negativity.

It's not easy, but I hope you will cultivate an awareness and appreciation for the full spectrum of life's experiences. Like I shared earlier, we all have setbacks. We have ups and downs, and that's okay. Just do your best. We need to experience the doubts, fears, pain, sadness, and other challenging parts of life in order to savor the many positive aspects. So be brave, and do hard things. It's all part of living life to its fullest.

> "For what it's worth, it's never too late to be whoever you want to be. I hope you live a life you're proud of, and if you find you're not, I hope you have the strength to start over."
> —*F. Scott Fitzgerald*

Finally, I hope you will do your very best to just be your beautiful, exceptional self. Don't try to impress anyone or concern yourself with what others may or may not think of you, including me. Don't ever compare. And don't be afraid to stray from well-trodden paths. Be different. As Vincent van Gogh said, "Normality is a paved road: It's comfortable to walk, but no flowers grow." So be true to yourself and strike out in your own direction to experience the endless beauty of this wonderful world. It's all out there just waiting for you to bear witness. Each of you is a unique and special person. Let your light shine brightly. I wish you could see yourself through my eyes. I'm so proud of you. You fill my heart with love and gratitude.

Thank you for joining me on this tour of my garden. Serving as your guide has been a blessing and a privilege. I hope you enjoyed the outing as much as I did, and that you could feel the positive energy and wishes in my words. I want nothing but the very best for you, which is exactly what you deserve.

Namaste.

> "What you are is what you have been.
> What you'll be is what you do now."
> —*Buddha*

Proud of You
by IN-Q

I don't need to know you to be proud of you
I'm proud of you
For all you've done and all you do
Because you're trying to become a better version of you
And fucking I'm proud of you

PROUD OF YOU

I hope this poem will empower you
I hope that you'll remember it, the next time someone is doubting you
I hope that you'll remember it, the next time them, is you
And you're doubting yourself cause you have nothing else to do
Pull the voice inside, aside, you're on their side, look them in the eyes
    and say . . .

Who are you to talk to you that way?!

You wouldn't let another person talk to you that way,
So what makes you think that just because it's you, it's okay?
You probably never talk to another person that way,
You'd either walk away, or defend yourself if you stayed
But since you're that other person in this particular case,
And you can't leave yourself, you have to learn to hold the space
So say "I'm proud of you"
Even if it feels like it's pretend
Try talking to yourself like you're your own best friend
Try talking to yourself like the relationship could end
And the words you choose have consequence

Don't take yourself for granted just because you're always there
Celebrate yourself for always being there
Always being here
Compliment the mirror
Let's be clear, self-help is self care

Are you aware that your awareness and your ego are completely different things?
Are you scared of the dichotomy constructing everything?
Are you prepared to share the inner space without defining things?
Are you attached to the illusion and the lullaby it sings?
Are you distracted by the story, even if it isn't true?
Cause if you are, you're not alone, it happens to me, too
And still I'm proud to be proud of you

Yea, you
The infinite you

PROUD OF YOU

The nonspecific you
The specifically terrific you
The universal you
The perfectly imperfect you
Look at you
You eternal you
You raced against at least 100 million sperm before becoming you and you and you

The one and only life will make
You have some nerve to walk around like you're some sort of mistake
You deserve to walk around like you're designed to take up space
Like you're aligned from the core inside the earth to outer space
You're a fucking miracle
Without a molecule to waste

You're a physical expression of fate and I relate
You're a mystical expression of fate and we relate
You're a musical, magical, beautiful, powerful individual
That's why I'm extra proud of you even when you get cynical

Remember that when times are tough
Close your eyes and hear my voice, you're a million times enough
Close your eyes and hear your voice
Until it's something you can trust

You're a million times enough
You're a million times enough
You're a million times enough
You're a million times enough

You are the sum of all of your experiences
You are the sum of none of your experiences

You're only you because they doubted you

You're alive and I'm proud of you

RECOMMENDED READING

If you are looking for more information on the subjects introduced in *Welcome to My Garden*, the following books are a great place to start. They all left their mark on me in some fashion. Hopefully they will do the same for you.

Accept This Gift: Selections from a Course in Miracles by Helen Schucman
The Alchemist by Paulo Coelho
The Almanack of Naval Ravikant: A Guide to Wealth and Happiness by Eric Jorgenson
The Art of Happiness: A Handbook for Living by the Dalai Lama and Howard C. Cutler, MD
The Art of Living by Thích Nhất Hạnh
Atomic Habits: An Easy & Proven Way to Build Good Habits & Break Bad Ones by James Clear
The Blue Zones Secrets for Living Longer: Lessons from the Healthiest Places on Earth by Dan Buettner
The Body Keeps the Score: Brain, Mind, and Body in the Healing of Trauma by Bessel van der Kolk
The Book of Joy: Lasting Happiness in a Changing World by the Dalai Lama and Desmond Tutu
The Boy, the Mole, the Fox and the Horse by Charlie Mackesy
The Creative Act: A Way of Being by Rick Rubin
Essence of the Bhagavad Gita: A Contemporary Guide to Yoga, Meditation & Indian Philosophy by Eknath Easwaran
Essence of the Dhammapada: The Buddha's Call to Nirvana by Eknath Easwaran
Essence of the Upanishads: A Key to Indian Spirituality by Eknath Easwaran

RECOMMENDED READING

Factfulness: Ten Reasons We're Wrong About the World—and Why Things Are Better Than You Think by Hans Rosling, Anna Rosling Rönnlund, and Ola Rosling

The Four Agreements: A Practical Guide to Personal Freedom by Don Miguel Ruiz

Four Thousand Weeks: Time Management for Mortals by Oliver Burkeman

Inquire Within: Poems by IN-Q

Letters to My Son: A Father's Wisdom on Manhood, Life, and Love by Kent Nerburn

Living from the Soul: The 7 Spiritual Principles of Ralph Waldo Emerson by Sam Torode

Loving What Is: Four Questions That Can Change Your Life by Byron Katie

Man's Search for Meaning by Viktor E. Frankl

The Measure of My Days: One Woman's Vivid, Enduring Celebration of Life and Aging by Florida Scott-Maxwell

The Miracle of Mindfulness: An Introduction to the Practice of Meditation by Thích Nhất Hanh

The Monk Who Sold His Ferrari: A Fable about Fulfilling Your Dreams & Reaching Your Destiny by Robin Sharma

The Obstacle is the Way by Ryan Holiday

The Power of Now: A Guide to Spiritual Enlightenment by Eckhart Tolle

The Road Less Traveled: A New Psychology of Love, Traditional Values, and Spiritual Growth by M. Scott Peck, MD

The Ruthless Elimination of Hurry: How to Stay Emotionally Healthy and Spiritually Alive in the Chaos of the Modern World by John Mark Comer

Small Graces: The Quiet Gifts of Everyday Life by Kent Nerburn

Stillness is the Key by Ryan Holiday

Think and Grow Rich by Napoleon Hill

Think Like a Monk: Train Your Brain for Peace and Purpose Every Day by Jay Shetty

A Thousand Names for Joy: Living in Harmony with the Way Things Are by Byron Katie

The Untethered Soul: The Journey Beyond Yourself by Michael A. Singer

Walden: or, Life in the Woods by Henry David Thoreau

The War of Art: Break Through the Blocks and Win Your Inner Creative Battles by Steven Pressfield

ACKNOWLEDGMENTS

Welcome to my Garden was written for my children, so I'd first like to acknowledge their wonderful mothers, Tricia and Sharon, who deserve far more credit than I do for raising some truly amazing kids. They blessed me with the most precious gift imaginable when they brought these beautiful souls into the world and allowed me to be a part of their lives. I'll always be more grateful than words can adequately express.

While writing *Welcome to My Garden*, I was touched by the unexpected support, encouragement, and love from friends, colleagues, and family (including my kids). Many of these people reviewed draft chapters and, in some cases, the entire manuscript, offering valuable feedback along the way. Perhaps more importantly, every time I had doubts about the project or felt unsure of myself, the universe seemed to put someone in my path who provided timely encouragement and support. It was a pleasant surprise that the creation process would be influenced by so many people. As such, I'd like to thank Angel Trinidad, Brandon Turner, Cole Kline, Elliot Snook, Jae Park, Kara Beckmann, Lisa Van Der Merwe, Micah Cabagbag, Mike Williams, Ryan Murdock, Seva Partney, Todd Murray, Tricia Murray, Cody Vlaun, and Walker Meadows.

In terms of the editorial and design process, I was blessed to work with a talented team of professionals who played important roles in bringing the project to fruition. I'd first like to thank my brilliant developmental editor and project director, Maria Gagliano. This is the second time I've had the privilege of working with Maria, and it

ACKNOWLEDGMENTS

was another wonderful experience. Maria has a way of bringing out the best in me and deserves credit for making this book far better than I could have ever managed on my own. She provided the perfect combination of encouragement and direction, recognizing when I was holding back and challenging me to be vulnerable, share my feelings, and stay true to my audience and myself. When I made the decision to self-publish, Maria also assembled an outstanding team, including copyeditor Elizabeth Blachman, cover and interior designer Karl Spurzem, and proofreader Dan Avant. I'm immensely grateful for their respective contributions.

Thank you to my friend and gifted writer IN-Q for granting permission to share one of his amazing poems, "Proud of You." IN-Q is a true master of his craft and a special person. His work resonates with me, and his book *Inquire Within* is a treasure.

As mentioned in the opening letter, the conviction to write *Welcome to My Garden* came on my trip to Nepal and was influenced by the conversations and relationships that emerged on the trek to Everest Base Camp. It was a life-changing experience that was made possible by a special group of trekkers and guides. I would like to thank the following people who each played a role in making this such a memorable and impactful trip: Angel Trinidad, Avery Stumm, Brad Griffith, Cody Kline, Cole Kline, Dreama Walton, Dylan Blecher, Elliot Snook, Florence Zhu, Geljen Sherpa, John Jones, Dr. Jon Kedrowski, Kelly Jensen, Lakpa Sherpa, Luis Neto, Maggie Woods, Michael Kelly, Nino Lintermo, Russ Perry, and Sheldon Blake. A special thank you to my friend Mike Posner, who was not only one of the orchestrators of the trip but made it a transformational experience and voiced his support for this project. Mike is an extraordinary individual who inspires me and makes the world a better place.

I'd like to thank my partners at Open Door Capital (Chapter 2) for their continued friendship and support, including cofounders Brandon Turner and Ryan Murdock and the rest of the general partners, including Walker Meadows, Jae Park, Micah Cabagbag, Michelle Oppelt,

ACKNOWLEDGMENTS

Mike Williams, and Sydney Barker. This is a special team of humans that I'm grateful to be a part of.

I'd also like to acknowledge the friends I mentioned in Chapter 3 who showed up to surprise and support me for my first ultramarathon: Nate Robbins, Ashley Kehr, Serena Norris, Mike Nuss, Alex Schauer, Alex Camacho, AJ and Tessa Osborne, Ashley Wilson, Kara Beckmann, Ryan and Pinky Murdock, Brandon and Heather Turner, Tyler Combs, Charles McKinney, and Brittany Arneson. I met these wonderful people through a Maui Mastermind group, and their gesture was meaningful to me. I'm also grateful to my running coach, Ian Sharman, whose guidance helped me overcome my limiting beliefs and achieve feats of endurance I didn't think were possible.

Much of this book was written while sitting on a comfortable, red sofa in the back corner of the Panacea Coffee House & Café in Waynesville, North Carolina's historic Frog Level. The sofa faces a large bank of windows, through which I could enjoy the greenery and watch the waters of Richland Creek flow by as I labored over this project. I'm grateful to proprietors Brian and Theresa Pierce for providing such a welcoming and peaceful environment where I could do my best work. If you're ever in Waynesville, be sure to stop in and enjoy the best cup of coffee in North Carolina.

Finally, I'd like to thank you, the reader, for purchasing this book and even more so for the gift of your precious time and attention. It is truly humbling and fills me with gratitude. I wish you all the very best.

ENDNOTES

1. Charlotte Hilton Andersen, "Feeling Thankful Can Help Prevent These 7 Major Diseases, Says Research," *The Healthy*, November 28, 2022, https://www.thehealthy.com/habits/how-to-prevent-disease-with-gratitude-from-doctors/.
2. "New Survey: One in Five Americans Are Spiritual but Not Religious," A joint study by Florida State University and the Public Religion Research Institute (PRRI), November 6, 2017, https://www.prri.org/press-release/new-survey-one-five-americans-spiritual-not-religious/.
3. "Mindfulness for Your Health: The Benefits of Living Moment by Moment," *NIH News in Health*, June 2021, https://newsinhealth.nih.gov/2021/06/mindfulness-your-health.
4. Thích Nhất Hạnh, *The Miracle of Mindfulness: An Introduction to the Practice of Meditation* (Boston: Beacon Press, 1975).
5. Mayo Clinic Staff, "Positive Thinking: Stop Negative Self-Talk to Reduce Stress," Mayo Clinic, February 3, 2022, https://www.mayoclinic.org/healthy-lifestyle/stress-management/in-depth/positive-thinking/art-20043950.
6. Meghan K. Edwards and Paul D. Loprinzi, "Experimental effects of brief, single bouts of walking and meditation on mood profile in young adults," *Health Promotion Perspectives*, July 7, 2018, 8(3): 171–178, doi: 10.15171/hpp.2018.23, https://www.ncbi.nlm.nih.gov/pmc/articles/PMC6064756/; Gregory N. Bratman et al., "Nature Experience Reduces Rumination and Subgenual Prefrontal Cortex Activation," *Proceedings of the National Academy of Sciences*, 112, no. 28, July 2015, 8567-72. doi:10.1073/pnas.1510459112, https://www.pnas.org/doi/abs/10.1073/pnas.1510459112.

ABOUT THE AUTHOR

Brian Murray is an entrepreneur, business executive, and author. He is cofounder of Open Door Capital, a private equity firm with more than $1B in assets under management. He is also the founder of Washington Street Properties, which was ranked on the Inc. 5000 list of the nation's fastest-growing private companies for five consecutive years.

Brian is the author of *Crushing It in Apartments and Commercial Real Estate*, which garnered multiple book awards, and coauthor of *The Multifamily Millionaire*, Volumes I & II. He has been interviewed and quoted by dozens of major media outlets including CNN, MarketWatch, PBS, the *Wall Street Journal*, and the *New York Times*.

Brian resides in western North Carolina, where he spends time working on his ranch, working on himself, reading, writing, hiking, and trail running in the Great Smoky Mountains.

Made in the USA
Columbia, SC
15 December 2023